THE ADVENTURE GUIDE
TO ITALY

Michael H. Sedge

THE
ADVENTURE
GUIDE
TO
ITALY

Michael H. Sedge

MPC
HUNTER
PUBLISHING INC

Hunter Publishing, Inc.
300 Raritan Center Parkway
Edison NJ 08818
(201) 225 1900

ISBN 1-55650-068-8

Printed in Singapore through Palace Press

Photographs: Strawberry Media

Cover photograph: Alleghe, near Belluno (Fotocolor
E.N.I.T.—Roma)

Published in the UK by:
Moorland Publishing Co. Ltd.
Moor Farm Road, Airfield Estate
Ashbourne, Derbyshire DE6 1HD
England

ISBN 086190-246-7

CONTENTS

This book is for Harry Sedge, who stimulated my interest in the outdoors and guided me through many adventures. The memories of Michigan outings will live with me forever.

This dedication would not be complete without also including Joyce Sedge, who supported our year-round ventures, often joining in though she may have preferred to be elsewhere.

I love you both.

Acknowledgements

My sincere thanks to all those who assisted in making this book a reality, especially Diego Burla; Massimo Canevarolo; Angelo D'Arrigo; Andrea Maria Nesler; Sergio Serafini; Beppe Tenti; and Pier Carlo Toffoletti. A very special thank you to Curzio Casoli; Enzo Maolucci and Franco Tassi. Their assistance was invaluable.

Important

Information in this book is subject to change without notice. This statement is particularly important with regard to Italy, where overnight changes are common. Trails, roads and whole parks may close; public transportation services may be suspended or rerouted; office addresses and telephone numbers may change. When in doubt, call one of the tourist offices listed in Appendix C. They normally keep track of changes that might affect visitors. Be prepared to play it by ear if need be and take things as they come. Matters that may seem simple elsewhere are often fraught with adventure in Italy, even for those who live here.

Because fees and prices change frequently—generally upward—we have, in most cases, avoided listing precise figures.

If you should come upon changes during your travels, we would appreciate it if you would let us know. This will insure that future editions are as up-to-date as possible. Your cooperation will help us as well as fellow adventurers.

INTRODUCTION

Italy. Land of the Roman Empire. Land of artistic genius. Land of fine wines. Land of the pizza. For centuries Italy has been associated with and recognized for its history, art and cuisine. Yet, there is another side.

Over the past 14 years I have enjoyed some of the finest alpine trekking in Europe, hiked through breathtaking land-scapes, explored volcanoes as they belched molten lava, toured historical sites on a bicycle laden with camping gear, paddled ancient rivers, climbed mountain heights and explored echoing caves far below the earth's surface. I have assisted in archaeological digs and explored sunken cities with scuba gear. In an outdoor survival school, I faced the wilds with nothing but the clothes on my back. In flowing mountain streams I discovered flakes of gold. I have even parachuted from mountain peaks and lived to tell the tale. All of this, and more, without leaving Italy.

When you come to Italy, come to add another chapter in your logbook of travel adventure. This is the perfect country to do so. As I discovered, Italy offers everything an adventurer could desire.

One of the major problems facing foreign adventurers has always been making connections. They come to Italy and, too often, spend weeks finding out what to do and where to go. The following chapters should eliminate that problem. In addition to the general information, the references provided will allow you to determine what adventures you wish to enjoy and set them up prior to your departure.

Italy is a unique and beautiful country. Enjoy its history, its art and its fine cuisine. Above all, enjoy its adventure.

PART I

ITALIAN INSIGHT

Geography

Italy is a 700-mile/1,127-kilometer peninsula extending into the Mediterranean. It has an area of 116,303 square miles (301,225 square kilometers). On the west and south it includes the large islands of Sardinia and Sicily, Pantelleria, and the Eolian (Lipori) group. Throughout history, Italy's position on the main routes between Europe, Africa, and the Orient has given it great political, economic, and strategic importance. The peninsula is 43 miles (69 kilometers) from Albania, and Sicily is 90 miles (145 kilometers) from the African mainland.

Except for the Po Valley in the north, and small coastal areas, Italy is rugged and mountainous. The climate is generally mild and Mediterranean, but there are wide variations. Sicily and the south are comparable to southern California, though warmer on the average. The Alps and Dolomites in the north have a climate similar to Colorado.

Italy is divided into 20 regions, each with a capital city. Each region has its own gastronomy, traditions, and adventures.

Regions of Italy

1. Piedmont
2. Aosta Valley
3. Liguria
4. Lombardy
5. Trentino-Alto Adige
6. Veneto
7. Friuli-Venezia Giulia
8. Emilia Romagna
9. Marche
10. Tuscany
11. Umbria
12. Latium
13. Campania
14. Abruzzi
15. Molise
16. Apulia
17. Basilicata
18. Calabria
19. Sicily
20. Sardinia

Climate

It rains about 80 days a year in Italy, for an average rainfall of nearly 30 inches (760 millimeters). There are periods of more intense rainfall in October, November and December. July and August are the lowest rainfall months. It is still advisable to pack a raincoat, however.

Winter is rather windy in Italy. In the south, temperatures are mild, and far from unpleasant. The central part of the peninsula experiences cold wind and frequent drizzles, while there are often snow and bitter temperatures in the north.

The average monthly temperatures in Fahrenheit (Centigrade in parenthesis) are: January, 46° (7.5° C); February, 48° (8.8° C); March 51° (10.8° C); April, 58° (14.2° C); May, 65° (18.2° C); June, 72° (22.3° C); July, 77° (24.9° C); August, 77° (24.6° C); September, 70° (21.3° C); October, 62° (16.8° C); November, 55° (12.8° C); December, 48° (8.7° C).

History

Modern Italian history dates from 1870 with unification of the entire peninsula under King Victor Emmanual II of the House of Savoy. From 1870 until 1922, Italy was a constitutional monarchy with a parliament elected under limited suffrage.

During World War I, Italy denounced its standing alliance with Germany and Austria-Hungary and in 1915 entered the war on the side of the Allies. Under the postwar settlement, Italy received some former Austrian territory along the northeast frontier. In 1922, Benito Mussolini came to power and, in the course of the next few years, eliminated the old political parties, curtailed personal liberties, and installed a Fascist dictatorship called the Corporate State. The King, with little or no power, remained titular head of state.

World War II found Italy allied with Germany. Italy declared war on the United Kingdom and France in 1940. Following the Allied invasion of Sicily in 1943, Italy became a co-belligerent of the Allies against Germany. A noteworthy popular resistance movement was conducted, especially in central and northern Italy, against the remaining Germans, who finally were driven out in April 1945. The monarchy was ended by a plebiscite in 1946, and a constituent assembly was elected to draw up the plans for the republic.

Under the 1947 peace treaty, minor adjustments were made in Italy's frontier with France; the eastern border area was transferred to Yugoslavia; and the area around the city of Trieste was designed as a free territory. In 1954, the free territory, which had remained under the administration of U.S. and U.K. forces (Zone A, including the city of Trieste) and Yugoslav forces (Zone B), was divided between Italy and Yugoslavia, principally along the zonal boundary. This arrangement was made permanent by the Italian-Yugoslav Treaty of Osimo, ratified in 1977. Under the peace treaty, Italy also gave up its overseas territories and certain Mediterranean islands.

People

The Italians are a people of tradition. Not Greek tradition, not French, Dutch, German, Spanish, or even Italian. Rather, they are a combination of them all. They have been a population passed between barbarians, emperors, and kings. Each new conqueror and ruling people added characteristics that helped form the country's vast and varied culture.

Today Italy is booming industry in the north, ski resorts in the Alps, centers of ancient tradition in the tourist-filled streets of Florence and Venice, a capital of Christianity in Rome, a headquarters for southern European NATO forces in Naples, a growing seaport in Bari, and a rich agricultural region in Sicily. Mingled among the bustling cities are out-of-the-way villages and towns that never seem to change. It is these places and the simple people that live there that keep the true spirit of Italy somewhat apart from the modern world. They are proud people, with strong family ties and a love for life.

Taormina street music and dancing.

Italy has the fifth highest population density in Europe—about 490 persons per square mile (200 per square kilometer). Minority groups are small, the largest being the German-speaking people of the Bolzano province and the Slovenes around Trieste. Other groups are the ancient communities of Albania, Greek, Ladino, and French origin. Roman Catholicism is the official religion—99% of the people are nominally Catholic—but all religious faiths are provided equal freedom by the constitution, and one can find most religions practiced here.

Entering Italy

A passport is required to visit Italy, unless you are a citizen of a Common Market nation, in which case a valid I.D. card is sufficient. Upon entry into the country you are automatically registered—by your hotel or customs authorities—onto the tourist roster of the local police station. Your tourist status enables you to remain in Italy without a visa for up to 3 months.

Should you decide to extend your visit you must obtain a permission document ("Permesso di Soggiorno") from the Foreigner's Office ("Ufficio Stranieri") of the central police headquarters in your area.

Money Matters

You can change money at most Italian banks. They are open from 8:30 a.m. to 1:30 p.m. Monday through Friday. Personal checks are rarely cashed unless you have some form of account already established with the bank. While changing foreign currency into Italian lire is usually no problem, converting lire into another currency, U.S. dollars for example, is rarely possible and never without a receipt from the bank where you originally changed your money.

You can also change money at one of the many "cambio" offices located in airports, train stations, and major cities.

These are international money dealers and you will often find better exchange rates here than in banks.

There are no restrictions on the amount of foreign currency you may bring into Italy. Amounts exceeding 1,000,000 lire, however, must be reported at the border or airport where you enter, and a V2 declaration form filed. Tourists may not import or export more than 400,000 lire in Italian currency.

Telephones

You will not find many telephone booths, particularly in the suburbs. Fortunately, just about every bar and restaurant has a public telephone. Telephone slugs, called "gettoni," are used exclusively in some telephones. Newer public telephones also use 100 and 200 lire coins. "Gettoni," costing 200 lire each, can usually be purchased from the cashier in the establishment you are calling from. If the word "teleselezione" is printed on the phone, after inserting a sufficient number of slugs or coins, you can make direct international calls by using the country code prefix (United States and Canada, 001; Great Britain, 0044; Eire, 00353).

To call Brooklyn, for example, you would insert a sufficient amount of money into the telephone box, dial 00 (international prefix) 1 (North America code number) 718 (area code for Brooklyn) and the home number.

If you are calling from a non-teleselezione telephone or wish to call person-to-person, collect, or reverse the charges, you must place the call through the international operator by dialing 170.

If you want more peace and quiet than can be found in a bar, or if you can't find a sufficient amount of change or slugs, you can go to the Public Telephone Posts (PTP) offices. These are found in major cities as well as airports and train stations.

Public Transportation

Most major international airlines have service to Rome and

Milan. Jet service to the United States, Canada and Great Britain is daily.

Public transportation throughout Italy is modern, efficient, and reasonably priced. Most major cities have good subway systems. Meter taxis are inexpensive and usually available at stands. Unmetered taxis should be avoided. Bus service is excellent in most cities and suburbs. Many minor towns, and mountain areas, are reached exclusively by bus.

The best way to get from one city to another is by train. The Italian State Railways have made available special 1st and 2nd class, reduced-rate tourist tickets for foreign travelers. These tickets may be purchased on presentation of a passport or other document—such as military or Common Market I.D. cards— at authorized travel agencies, frontier posts and Italy's international airports. The tickets are valid for 8, 15, 21 or 30 days and entitle the holder to travel without restrictions on the entire Italian railway network. With this ticket you do not have to pay any fast train ("rapidi") supplements.

Italy maintains an extensive motorway system. Non-Europeans who plan to drive in the country should obtain an international driving license from their city motor vehicle office before leaving for Italy. If you plan to rent a car—most major rental companies are found in Italy—you can take advantage of tow assistance packages: the "Pacchetto Italia" and the "Pacchetto Italia-Sud," that are available from automobile associations and the Italian National Tourist Offices in the United States, Canada, United Kingdom and Eire. The "Pacchetto Italia" contains coupons for a discount on about 35 gallons of gasoline (150 liters) and for discounts on highway tolls (both of which are expensive compared to other countries). The "Pacchetto Italia-Sud," which can be used in Lazio, Abruzzo and other regions of the south (including Sicily and Sardinia), offers more gas-coupons as well as other coupons for highway use.

Before leaving for Italy it is a good idea to write or call the nearest Italian National Tourist office and ask about these and other benefits for tourists. Offices in the United States are located at: 360 Post Street, Suite 801, San Francisco, CA 94108, tel. (415) 392–6206; 500 North Michigan Avenue, Chicago, IL 60611, tel. (312) 644–0990; 630 Fifth Avenue, Suite 1565, New York, NY 10111, tel. (212) 245–4822. In Canada: 3 Place Ville-Marie, Suite 22, Montreal 113, Que., tel. (514) 866–7667. In Great Britain: 1 Princess Street, London W1 8AY, tel. (01) 408–1254. And in Eire: 47 Merrion Square, Dublin 2, tel. (01) 766–397.

Post Offices

All Italian post offices are open 6 days a week between 8:30 a.m. and 2 p.m., central offices until 8 p.m.. Post offices are easily recognized by the PT ("posta telegrafo") signs displayed outside.

There are windows for the various services such as stamps, money orders, and telegrams. Long lines are a trademark of Italian post offices. If lines are too long, you can also purchase envelopes, postcards and postage stamps at many tobacco ("tabacchi") shops displaying a large white letter "T" on a black background outside the store.

Accommodations

Sleeping out in the open under the stars can be romantic and is certainly economical, but it is not always healthy— particularly in the winter or in city environments. There are, however, a number of alternatives to fit any budget.

Hostels, student houses and other hotel facilities intended for young people (under 26) can be found in various cities throughout the country. Because these are very inexpensive, it is sometimes difficult to find an empty bed; you should make reservations far in advance. Some places that offer youth accommodations require a card from the Italian Hotel Association for Youths (A.I.G.), International Youth Federation (I.Y.H.F.) or a student identification card. And most places limit the duration of your stay to 3 consecutive nights.

For more information on youth accommodations in Italy, write: AIG National Headquarters, Palazzo della Civiltà del Lavoro, (EUR), 00100 Rome, Italy.

There is an abundance of hotels and boarding houses suited to all tastes and pocket-books. Usually those who are on tight budgets will find the III and IV class establishments more accessible. Although they may not offer the latest in modern conveniences, most are clean and friendly. For a complete listing of hotels in the area you will be visiting, write to the Provincial Board for Tourism. If you do not know the exact address merely write E.P.T. in the major city of the region (for example, "E.P.T., Florence, Italy"). Another option would be to write the Regional Tourist Office (addresses are located in Appendix C). The hotel list they provide includes addresses, telephone numbers, classes, services offered, and price ranges. With this you can easily make advance bookings by telephone, telegram, or letter.

There are many boarding houses, or pensions, in Italy that offer meals and accommodations. If you sign up for half pension, you'll receive one meal (normally dinner) for each day you remain. If you ask for full pension, you'll get a room, small breakfast, lunch and dinner.

The price of hotels and pensions sometimes includes state tax, known as IVA. Be sure to inquire whether or not it is included. If not, you can expect to pay an additional 18% of the daily rate.

In 1965 the National Association of Agriturist was established in Rome to promote farm lodging for vacationers. Since that time, Agriturist has grown to include some of the finest and cheapest accommodations throughout the peninsula and major islands. This type of lodging is similar to the bed-and-breakfast accommodations found in other countries and is highly recommended, not only for economical reasons but because it will allow you to get to know the true people of Italy. The current Agriturist directory contains more than 1,600 equipped camping facilities and farm, home and apartment lodgings ranging in price from 5,000 to 25,000 lire per night, many including meals.

Since many of Agriturist's lodgings are located in the areas of high adventure, this is something you may want to look into. For a current directory (in 3 languages, including English) write Agriturist, Corso Vittorio Emanuele, 101, 00186 Rome, Italy.

Most adventurers come to Italy with camping in mind, and rightly so. Italy is honeycombed with fine camping facilities with mobile-home, trailer, and tent accommodations. Rates vary according to location and season, but are very reasonable. From October through April many camping facilities in areas where summer tourism is heavy are completely booked. So it is best to call or write in advance. You can locate camping facilities in the yellow pages of the telephone directory under "Campeggio." You can also write to the regional tourist board for a listing of campsites. The Touring Club Italiano (TCI) and Automobile Club of Italy (ACI) publish a comprehensive booklet of campsites and tourist villages throughout the country.

Camping, one of the cheaper ways to see Italy.

This can be purchased at bookstores or directly from TCI offices (locations and telephone numbers are found in Appendix E).

"Euro Camping Italy and Corsica" is another good guide to campsites put out each year in three languages by Editoriale Eurocamp, Via G. Prati 2, 20145 Milano. Cost is about US $10.

For free information regarding camping in Italy write to the Centro Internazionale Prenotazioni Campeggio, Casella Postale 649, 50100 Florence, Italy.

Dining

Better to forget about the typical ham and egg breakfast; it's not part of the Italian way of life and difficult to come by. The vast majority of Italians, before going to work, enter a bar and order a "cappuccino" (coffee and milk) and a "cornetto" (a sweet roll in the shape of horns). If you want, you can repeat the ritual several times during the morning—the Italians often do.

There are many fine restaurants in Italy. The cooking is always good and many places have special dishes, and local wines, which should be tried.

In addition to restaurants, which normally have long menus, there are many family-run establishments, or trattorie, that offer limited selections. These popular places cost less and have excellent food. Most often, trattorie will have daily specials only.

In the evening many trattorie serve pizza. The pizza, together with spaghetti, is the symbol of Italian cooking; alone it can be a complete and inexpensive evening meal.

A few more tips on restaurant eating: bread ("pane") is served with all meals—except pizza—and is added to the final bill ("conto"), whether it has been touched or not. Therefore, if you do not desire bread, simply tell the waiter. Wine, the fountain of Italian youth, is available in all eating establishments. Most places have major brands of bottled wine, but house wine (vino della casa) often costs less and is very good. When you are ready for the bill, ask the waiter. There is normally a fixed cover charge of 15%.

Be sure that you receive a receipt which contains the restaurant's name and tax code ("codice fiscale" or "partita IVA"). Keep the receipt until you are 328 feet (100 meters) from the restaurant. It's Italian law. In the event that tax officials want to insure the establishment is not cheating on its taxes, they can ask you for the receipt. If you don't have it, you could be fined.

For a quick snack, Italy offers rotisseries and quick-food bars. Here there are no service charges; often you eat standing, resting your plate on a shelf. These places serve a wide variety of dishes, including spaghetti, chicken and pizza. The more characteristic foods are "crocchette" (small oblong balls of rice, potatoes, or ground meat, dipped in egg and bread crumbs and then fried), "calzoni" (a bread dough shell filled with ham and mozzarella cheese, baked in an oven), and "crostini" (slices of bread covered with mozzarella cheese and ham, baked in an oven.

Tuscan restaurant.

Adventure Tours

Though you may be adventuresome, taking on an unknown land, language, and culture can be a little too much to tackle at one time. Organized tours are a great way to overcome such obstacles. But don't think this means something on the level of sight-seeing by bus in Rome or a group visit to Pompeii. The tours you're after are true adventures.

In 1969, Mountain Travel was the first company to offer adventure vacations to exotic places like Nepal. Today there are more than 600 such outfitters offering tours throughout the world. Italy is no exception. Here you'll find organized alpine hikes, horseback trekking, freeclimbing, canoing, bicycle touring, spelunking, volcano exploration, diving, sled dog schools, outdoor survival training and more.

Organizations such as Trekking International, Hiking International, La Roncola and Bianca (detailed listings and addresses for these and others are provided in Appendix A) arrange special explorations and schools for English language adventurers each year. These operations take care of normal concerns like food and lodging, guides, maps, routes and, in many cases, equipment—and their fees are minimal.

Organized adventures are an excellent way to enjoy the natural beauty and excitement Italy offers, particularly if you are a newcomer to the country. Many of the succeeding chapters contain the names of outfitters that arrange outings in the areas covered in various chapters. Whether you eventually choose to join such groups is up to you. It is advisable, however, to take advantage of the list in Appendix A by writing for more information. That way you can see if the outings offered fit into your plans and would perhaps provide a safer, more enjoyable vacation.

Emergencies

An emergency could be anything from mechanical trouble on the road to injuries while traversing the Alps. Most often, however, emergencies come in the form of lost or stolen documents and personal possessions. Whatever the case, there may come a time when you need help.

For major emergencies and/or the loss of important items—passports, credit cards, traveler's checks—you should immediately contact the nearest consulate or embassy. The embassies of the United States, Canada, United Kingdom and Eire are located in Rome. Each country, however, maintains consulates in major cities like Milan, Florence and Naples.

Italy has a good emergency network through its telephone system. If you have car trouble, for example, simply dial 116 and you will automatically be connected to the Automobile Club d'Italia's road assistance office, which will immediately send out a tow-truck and mechanic. In the event of an injury, ambulance, Red Cross and police service can be obtained by dialing 113. A complete listing of embassy and emergency telephone numbers is found in Appendix B.

Most emergencies occurring on the trail fall under the jurisdiction of the Mountain Rescue Organization (CSA) or the Italian Alpine Club, whose members are trained and equipped for assisting adventurers in trouble. There are more than 350 Alpine Club offices throughout Italy. Prior to any major venture, it is suggested that you check into the nearest center for maps, advice, and to file a journey plan in case something does happen along the way.

There is another type of emergency that is often overlooked by vacationers until it happens. That is the emergency that occurs back home while you are in Italy. In this case, someone may need to contact you quickly. To do this, they will need to know where you are at all times. Provide them with telephone numbers if you know this information in advance. One of the easiest ways for family members to contact you while you are in Italy is through the Red Cross.

PART II

ITALY OUTDOORS

Nature conservation was written about by the ancient Romans. During the Renaissance, the alpine Forest of Cansiglio was declared a protected area by the Republic of Venice, with very severe penalties for anyone who endangered the zone. Today this tradition of conservation continues.

The first two Italian national parks, Abruzzo and Gran Paradiso, were created in 1922, and at that time the country seemed well attuned to the conservation of nature. But for political, cultural and economic reasons, after 1933 Italy did relatively little to save its natural environments for nearly 40 years.

It was only after 1970, the Year of European Conservation, that a new environmental attitude began to take shape. A growing conservation movement developed public concern about the urgent necessity for more protected areas, leading to significant steps by both national and local governments.

Today, thanks to the ceaseless efforts of the Committee for Italian National Parks and Equivalent Reserves, the World Wildlife Federation, and other protectionist organizations, the national government has developed and enlarged the existing national parks and created a considerable number of new re-

The Umbrian countryside.

Emblem of the Committee for Italian National Parks and Equivalent Reserves.

serves. At the same time, regional governments have begun taking concrete action to protect these zones. Though the administration of these protected areas is not always what it should be, in recent years the total area of the national parks has gone from 494,000 to 666,900 acres, with 148,200 acres of national reserves, 49,400 acres of wetlands and wildlife refuges, and 247,000 acres of regional parks. In 1971, the total budget for protected areas was 500 million lire. Now, more than 8,000 million lire is being spent.

According to the Italian Committee for National Parks and Equivalent Reserves, only 1.5% of Italy is currently protected. Their goal is to increase this to 10% by 1990. The figure is not excessive. Particularly when one considers that West Germany protects about 20% of its territory, Great Britain 10%, France 8%, Czechoslovakia and Yugoslavia 3%, and the United States, New Zealand and Japan, as well as various African nations such as Kenya, Tanzania, Rwanda and the Ivory Coast, about 10%.

Public opinion, especially among young people, seems very concerned about the goal of increasing Italy's natural environments. Eight new parks are expected in the near future. Some of these lie on the mainland, but two very important ones are located on islands: in Sicily (Etna, one of the most spectacular active volcanoes in Europe); and in Sardinia (mountains and coasts harboring the last mufflons, red deers, vultures and monk seals).

Protected Areas in Italy

There are currently 5 national parks in Italy: Stelvio and Gran Paradiso, located in the northern Alps; Circeo and Abruzzo, in the central area of the peninsula; and Calabria, specifically the Sila Mountain range at the toe of the Italian boot. These 5 parks account for nearly 667,000 acres of breathtaking meadows, forests, mountains, lakes, streams, and coastal environments. Here the adventurer will discover not only some of the nation's finest natural environments, but much of its wildlife and a variety of people, traditions and habitats. Detailed descriptions of Italy's national parks can be found later in this book.

In keeping with its goal to increase the overall protected lands in Italy, the Italian Committee for National Parks and Equivalent Reserves have proposed an additional eight new parks, covering 988,000 acres. Because several political approvals must be obtained before a national park can be officially sanctioned, it may be years before these areas carry the "National Park" title. In the meantime, however, several areas have been adapted for temporary use by hikers, cyclists, campers and all-round adventurists.

Besides Italy's national parks, there are 15 regional parks and another 25 under proposal. These offer excellent hiking and, in some cases, camping. Nature reserves in Italy currently number 25, with an additional 20 to be sanctioned. Several of these have been established by the World Wildlife Federation, while others are under the jurisdiction of UNESCO and other protective agencies.

Park Regulations

As in all protected areas, there are certain rules and regulations that must be followed in Italian parks and reserves. It is forbidden to: 1) leave designated trails or hiking routes; 2) start open fires—there are an average 700,000 countryside fires in Italy each year, causing 6,300 billion lire worth of damage; 3) camp in areas other than those designated; 4) discard garbage and other refuse; 5) disturb, molest or kill wildlife in any way; 6) damage, destroy, or remove nests, eggs or other elements of the natural environment, including plants and flowers; 7) bring dogs into protected areas, even if leashed; 8) carry arms of any type; 9) drive automobiles and/or motorcycles along undesignated routes.

Above all, park officials ask visitors to leave the environment as they found it.

Fauna

Despite what some people say—most often those who never leave the big cities—Italy has a vast variety of animal life. There are 105 mammal species found on the peninsula and neighboring islands, 230 species of birds, 30 amphibians, 51 reptiles, and 56 varieties of fish.

Brown bear, chamois, red and roe deer are all found here, as are wolf, wild cat, otter, marten, polecat, badger, fox, hares, moles, hedgehogs, marmot, weasel and squirrels. Some of the more unusual creatures one might encounter are wild boar and ibex.

There are many types of reptiles throughout the country: vipers, water snakes, slow-worms, both land and water tortoises and green lizards.

There is also a vast variety of birds, among them the golden eagle, the goshawk, the vulture, the eagle owl and the tawny owl.

A large percentage of the birds are found along the lakes and coastal areas. In the migratory seasons (spring and autumn)

Wildlife abounds in much of the Italian peninsula.

many water birds come to various parts of the country. Among the most important are the gray heron, the night heron, the stilt and the gull-billed tern. In the spring, autumn and winter you can often see cormorants, widgeons, teals, shovelers, pintails, mallards, garganeys, pochards and many waders.

The pride of Sardinia is the flamingo. On this Italian island, particularly in the provinces of Oristano and Cagliari, vast numbers of the pinkish-white birds can be found along the coasts and wetlands.

You will also find sea turtles, orca whales or even monk seals along Italy's coasts and encompassing seas. In the fresh water lakes and rivers live pike, sturgeon, rainbow trout, and other varieties.

Unfortunately, some of Italy's animal population is under threat of extinction. Of the 56 fish species, for example, 38 (or about 68%) are currently facing extinction. Thirty-eight percent of the nation's mammal population is threatened, 31% of the reptiles, 24% of the birds, and 20% of the amphibians.

Flora

From the northern Alps to the southern island of Sicily, Italy abounds with plant life. In the spring and summer the display of violet, crocus, blue moonwort, squill, aquilegia, gentian, lilly, wildflower, primrose, saxifrage, buttercup, orchid and innumerable other flowers, including some rare and unique varieties, is truly breathtaking. The vivid colors brighten the green glades and meadows and contrast sharply with the grays of the rocks and the large stretches of dark forests. There are endless birch woods on the high mountains, oak forests in the valleys, and pine on rocky terrain.

The country's national parks and wildlife reserves are excellent places to discover the various plant species. In the Abruzzo National Park, for instance, there are about 1,200 species of flowering plants. Sixty percent of the Gran Paradiso National Park is covered in forests of larch and spruce. Likewise, the National Park of Stelvio contains rich forests with

Colorful flora can be found in every part of the country.

similar species, in addition to cembran pine, Scotch pine and Swiss mountain pine.

Mediterranean evergreen shrubs, oaks, beech and birch forests are found in the southern regions of Italy, particularly around the Circeo, Abruzzo and Calabria National Parks as well as on the islands of Sicily and Sardinia.

Insects

As a result of marsh drainage and effective spraying with DDT immediately after World War II, Italy is no longer plagued with dangerous insects as in the past. Adventurers are more likely to encounter flies and mosquitoes which are a nuisance, rather than a danger. A good insect repellant should solve the problem. If you plan to sleep in the open, however, an insect net is a good idea.

Insects such as this dragonfly add to the color.

23

In addition to the bothersome insects, there is an array of beautiful and colorful insects as well. It is impossible to list all the insects that inhabit Italy, but there are species, particularly certain types of beetles typical of forest and mountain environments, that are scientifically very important. There are rhinoceros beetles, easily recognized by the characteristic horn; cerambix, with their long antennas; the colorful calosoma beetle; and such strange-looking insects as the walking stick, the praying mantis, and the oak leaf silk worm moth, whose wings look like a dried oak leaf.

Finding these and other tiny creatures calls for keen eyesight and an awareness of the habits of the insect world. It is often well worth the effort.

Rocks and Minerals

Because Italy contains many different geological structures, a variety of rocks and minerals exist here. Several minerals can be found in the volcanic zones of the south. In central and northern Italy, quartz and various collectible stones are present in streams and mountains. Italy, in fact, is one of the world's leading producers of marble, which in its natural state often contains a wide range of minerals.

Though the country is not exactly "rich" in gems and semiprecious stones, many do exist and have been found by collectors in the past. Most often these are found in the northern regions, and include diamond, ruby, sapphire, aquamarine, emerald, garnet, and zircon. In recent years, gold has also been discovered in several northern streams (see "Going for Gold" in Part XI).

Hunting and Fishing

To hunt in Italy, you must obtain authorization from officials of the region where you wish to hunt. Application is by written request—on Italian legal paper only. Include also 1) two copies of the written request, on normal paper; 2) an authenticated photocopy of an acceptable document of identification and a permit to carry arms for the purpose of hunting; 3) a photocopy of an insurance policy; 4) a deposit or an authenticated photocopy of a deposit made to the region's bank account—one must obtain the account number from the region—as a contribution towards the cost of game wardens and the restocking of game; 5) an official legal stamp valued at 3,000 lire.

Fishing is allowed in all fresh-water areas except where marked with prohibiting signs. You may obtain a 3-month temporary fresh-water fishing permit by presenting a request written on legal paper to the Assessorato Regionale alla Difesa dell'Ambiente in the region where you want to fish. In addition, the following documents are needed: 1) a deposit to the region's bank account to cover the fees and cost of the fishing permit; 2) official stamps to the value of 3,000 lire.

No permit is needed to fish in salt-water. Sport fishing in salt-water, however, can be done with individual gear only. Individual gear includes: 1) landing net or trawl net, the trawl net not exceeding 19.7 feet (6 meters) in length; 2) sweep-net, the perimeter of which cannot exceed 52 feet (16 meters); 3) fishing lines attached to rods, not more than 3 hooks per rod, and dead lines, not more than 6 hooks per line, (each fisherman is limited to 5 rods); 4) fixed or moveable tackle; 5) lines for dragging (surface or depth); 6) gaffs for surface fishing, underwater spearguns, harpoons for manual use, rods for octopus, squid and cuttlefish.

Sport fishing cannot be assisted by the use of lights of any kind, with the exception of torches or flashlights used during underwater or scuba fishing for safety reasons.

The sport fisherman may not exceed a daily limit of 11 pounds (5 kilograms) of fish, crustaceans, and/or mollusks, except in the case where a single fish exceeds the limit.

Underwater fishing, sport or professional, can be undertaken only without the use of underwater breathing equipment of any kind. Law permits the use of such equipment only for purposes other than fishing. Collection of coral or mollusks with the use of underwater breathing equipment is reserved for professional fishermen only. Underwater fishing is restricted to daylight hours.

Those wanting to hunt or fish in Italy should contact the Italian embassy or consulate nearest them 6 to 10 months before leaving, requesting assistance for fishing and/or hunting permits. There are also agencies in Italy which will handle the legal documentation required for a fee. One such agency which works almost exclusively with foreigners is Professional Assistance Service, Via Archimede 207, 00197 Rome, Italy.

Touring Club Italiano

Founded by a group of bicycle enthusiasts in 1894, the Touring Club Italiano for over three-quarters of a century has been engaged in the promotion of touring. It offers a means for getting to know Italy better through its monthly "Qui Touring" magazine, illustrated brochures, geographical, historical and artistic guides, road maps, and an international atlas. Of special interest to the adventurer are the National Park map series, which includes detailed hiking routes as well as information on flora, fauna and local history. Also very popular is the bicycle itinerary route series.

TCI also plans holiday tours—including outdoor vacations during the summer months—for students and groups interested in culture outings, holiday villages, camping and sailing courses. In addition the club issues snow bulletins during the winter, posts signs in locations of interest to tourists and issues discount coupons to foreigners for the purchase of gasoline and oil.

Touring Club Italiano

Emblem of the Touring Club Italiano (TCI).

The TCI has offices in nearly 1,000 cities, with numerous representatives throughout the country. Members of the TCI can obtain discounts on many tours and pay special low fees for various sports activities in Italy. Membership is 45,000 lire a year or 112,000 lire for three years. One can join at any TCI office, or by writing to the headquarters in Milan (see Appendix E for addresses).

Italian Alpine Club

The Italian Alpine Club (CAI) was begun in 1863. Today CAI has more than 205,000 members, 395 chapters and 280 local offices, covering every part of the country. Through the years CAI's activities have expanded to include mountaineering, climbing, trekking, hiking, speleology, skiing, survival and rescue service.

The club operates more than 470 refuges and 140 shelters in Italy's mountain and wilderness regions, nearly 200 alpine and speleology rescue stations, 150 avalanche rescue and research centers, 155 schools for outdoor activity training and employs a staff of 400 instructors and more than 1000 guides. In addition, the CAI maintains wilderness and mountain trails throughout Italy, insuring that route indicators are easily visible and accurate.

Anyone can join the Italian Alpine Club by visiting or writing one of the offices listed in Appendix D. There is a small fee and 2 passport-sized photographs are required. Members re-

CLUB ALPINO ITALIANO

Emblem of the Club Alpino Italiano.

ceive insurance, special tour opportunities, club publications, free access to all chapters, use of club gear for special adventures, maps and discount accommodations at all CAI huts and refuges. Some sporting goods manufacturers also offer discounts to CAI members.

More than this, however, being a member of the Italian Alpine Club insures you will never have to attempt an adventure alone, unless you want to do so. It is the largest and most prestigious organization of adventurers in the country.

Italian Tourist Offices

Italy has an excellent network of tourist offices: national, regional, provincial and city. There are branch offices located in all major airports and train stations.

Many tourist offices have prepared itineraries for auto, bicycle and/or walking tours, as well as various brochures on activities in the jurisdiction they cover. Much of this information is in English. The tourist offices can also recommend adventure groups and clubs to anyone interested in specific activities such as hiking, canoeing, volcano exploring and horseback trekking.

Addresses for regional tourist offices in Italy can be found in Appendix C.

PART III

ADVENTURES AFOOT

If the ups and downs of mountain trails and picturesque forests lure you, Italy will seem a land of fantasy. Hiking, backpacking and trekking ventures in this exciting country are not your usual organized tours with bus transportation, first-rate hotels, meals and guides. What you will get here is the freedom of a true down-to-earth, under-the-stars, roughing-it adventure—though there are also hundreds of easy one-day walking routes to be found as well.

Italy offers some of the finest and most varied walking in Europe—from the gentle, mysteriously beautiful hills of Etruria with their picturesque walled towns and villages, to the dramatically eroded peaks of the Dolomites; from the splendid snowy skyline of the Gran Paradiso to the long ridge of the Apennines with their great diversity of flora, extensive views and, for mountains, fairly stable weather conditions; from the hot lava flows of Mount Etna to the wildlife-filled National Park of Calabria.

The relatively mild climate makes Italy a perfect location for year-round hiking and backpacking. Spring is the time for educational hiking. With the aid of local maps you can easily combine tourist sights with leisurely walks and secluded trails. During the summer months the northern regions with their beautiful streams and panoramic scenery will add breathtaking excitement to backpacking vacations. When fall rolls around, the colorful flora found in the central wooded areas, such as the famed National Park of Abruzzo, will have you wondering whether it is Italy you are exploring or Canada. And don't pack up your gear during the winter. This is the period when all warm-blooded birds, and hikers, head south. Though the nights can be cool, the warm sea-breezes off Sicily will keep you moving over the rolling hills for days.

During recent years Italians have become increasingly involved in hiking and camping. This makes things easier for those who head out with no set location to spend the night. In the rural towns, camp sites are often available (except in July and August, when they are booked solid). If your venture is through the mountain or woodland solitudes, simply pitching a tent or rolling out the sleeping bag will pose no problems—unless you nestle on a hill of Italian ants.

But what do you do when the sun goes down, you are 10 miles from the nearest campground and there is no wooded area or mountain in sight? If you are in the country—with no

Hiking is one of the best ways to explore Italy's out-of-doors.

homes around—you can be assured that pitching a tent is allowed. If, on the other hand, a farm or village is in the area, ask the landowner's permission. Nine times out of 10 you will be welcomed.

If you are interested in obtaining a complete listing of campsites in Italy, there is one available free of charge from the Federazione Italiana del Campeggio (Italian Camping and Caravaning Federation), Via G. Mameli 2, Florence, Italy.

As mentioned, possibilities for adventures afoot are abundant. Most veteran hikers, however, agree upon 4 or 5 locations as being the ultimate in beauty, history and walking pleasure. Beginning in the north-west, near the French and Swiss borders, is the Gran Paradiso National Park. Encompassing the 4 valleys of the Gran Paradiso Massif, this area contains some of Italy's finest alpine scenery and wildlife.

To the east, in the Brenta Dolomite mountains, is the Stelvio National Park. Hiking and trekking adventures here can be planned to fit any schedule—a few hours, a single day, a week or more. For extended alpine outings, you can explore 2 groups of mountains adjacent to the Brenta Dolomites: the Presanella and the Adamello ranges. In most cases, if a plan is laid out carefully, you can see the area in 7 days of easy walking.

In central Italy, the Abruzzo National Park offers thick forests, mountains, rivers and lakes, not to mention an abundance of wildlife. Here, too, routes can easily be combined to fit any schedule.

An unusual outing is found along the west-central coast within the borders of the National Park of Circeo. Here you confront not only forests and mountains, but the sea as well.

To the south, adventurers enjoy the mild climate and splendor of the National Park of Calabria, which is actually three separate areas stretching along the Sila Mountain range from Lake Cecita to the tip of the boot near Reggio Calabria.

While these are among the favorite walking areas, there are thousands of others.

Planning is the key to a successful backpacking or hiking vacation, particularly if you are not familiar with the Italian language. In planning your Italian venture, be sure to study local maps on the topography, get a forecast of the weather

31

conditions for the period in which you will be traveling, and know the locations of the nearest towns and police stations. Advise someone who is staying behind about the route you are planning to follow.

If you want to set out in the company of others, there are associations, such as the Italian Alpine Club, that specialize in organizing group outings. A few other choices—all excellent if you do not speak Italian—are Hiking International, Trekking International and La Roncola (addresses in Appendix A). If you sign up for one of the pre-planned backpacking ventures these outfits offer, a bilingual guide and often all the necessary gear come with the package.

Alpine Treks

The Alps, which stretch across northern Italy from east to west, offer some of the finest trekking in the world. Unlike hiking, which often involves short excursions and relatively easy walking, an alpine trek is likely to be an extended walk over mountains and paths where the traditional tourist never ventures.

Huts and Refuges

Management and maintenance of alpine huts is one of the most important tasks of the Italian Alpine Club (CAI). As a rule, huts are spaced every 6–12 miles (10–20 kilometers). Trekkers, therefore, have easy access to food, water and lodging. Thus, with some planning, you can travel light with relatively little concern for supplies.

Most huts are comparable to tiny hotels and have all the basic necessities (water, light, heat, food). Members of the Italian Alpine Club enjoy a 50% reduction on the price of lodging and 10–15% reduction on meals at all CAI operated huts. There are also a few privately owned establishments in the Alps.

Anyone can become a member of the Italian Alpine Club regardless of nationality. This can be done at any CAI office (see Appendix D). All that is required are 2 2x2-inch photographs.

When to Go

The hiking season is relatively short in the Alps. Generally huts are open from the end of June through September. The ideal time to go is mid-July, when most of the snow has melted and the August crowds have not yet appeared. During the month of August, huts are busy and if you arrive late you may find yourself sleeping on the floor. No one is ever turned away, however.

Clothing and Equipment

Though you will not need all the accoutrements of backpacking—stove, tent, sleeping bag—the proper gear is still important. A good pair of boots is essential. A rugged rather than light weight pair is recommended. They should have been previously broken-in. Be sure to have something that protects you against the sun on hot days, and clothing for warmth during cool evenings in the huts. Try to be versatile. Likewise, polypropylene underwear, which can double as a sleeping suit. A Gortex shell jacket can serve as an insulating layer over a wool shirt or sweater and provide protection against the rain.

Miscellaneous items are a matter of personal preference, but you should probably include toilet articles, a towel, knife, canteen, small first aid kit and slippers for the hut.

On the Trail

You need not be an experienced mountaineer to enjoy the Italian Alps. These are not wild or forbidding mountains. Paths are well defined and excellent maps are available in major cities. The flexibility offered by the hut and trail network is a real plus. You can take short, easy walks or long extended hikes. Many adventurers feel it's best not to have a definite itinerary. Rather, they suggest going one hut at a time, letting your level of fitness, your mood, your experience and the trail conditions dictate.

It is almost impossible to get lost, particularly if you stay on the trails. These are marked with either a paint slash and/or trail numbers. There are also signs at trail junctions.

Because mountain trails are so well defined, the route directions given in the following pages do not go into great detail. They are presented as guidelines for the trekker, indicating what to cover each day and where to stop for the night. If you plan to get off the main route indicated in the maps, be sure to acquire a good trail map before heading out.

The Aosta Valley

A world of pastures, of peaks, of flowers and animals, of sun and snow, an austere world yet full of tranquility: this is the Aosta Valley. From Gressoney to Courmayeur and Champorcher, the High Routes 1 and 2, which follow, will lead you through an alpine region with a wealth of tradition, history and above all natural beauty.

When one thinks of the Aosta Valley, images of high peaks such as Mont Blanc, Monte Rosa, the Matterhorn and the Gran Paradiso normally come to mind—a world reserved for mountaineers and rock climbers. Yet there exist thousands of other possibilities for those who merely want to walk in the mountains. Paths and mule tracks extend for miles, ancient roads connect adjacent valleys, villages and alpine pastures.

The High Routes of the Aosta Valley cover 175 miles (282 kilometers) of beauty, not to mention the numerous sidetracks possible. The High Routes intersect and join numerous other paths which cross the Valley lengthwise, forming a rich and varied network of itineraries.

The Aosta Valley, one of Italy's most picturesque areas.

High Route symbols. In the example, High Route 1 and High Route 2, with Sidepath 3.

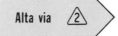

Marked road signs.

Alta via

Directional indicator.

6 **Lac Ner** 2530 m		15 min
7 **Fenêtre de Champorcher** 2826 m	1h	10 min
13 **Lillaz** 1617 m	4h	25 min
15 **Cogne** 1545 m	5h	10 min

Directional indicator with walking time. Destinations are indicated by name and number. Place names separated by a horizontal line (lower sign) are on a route branching off the main path taken.

30 **Torrent** 2179 m	1h	20 min
31 **Col Fenêtre** 2840 m	3h	15 min
38 **Planaval** 1554 m	9h	
Valgrisenche 1664 m	6h	25 min

Place name indicator.

Route Indicators found in the Italian Alps.

The main routes are well marked with triangle signs indicating 1 or 2. If you get off onto a side-path, you will find signs with a large number as well as a smaller "path number" below it. For example, a large 1, indicating the High Route 1, and under that number a tiny 3, indicating side-path number 3. Directional indicators with walking times are also found at itinerary crossings.

The normal route and most of the side-paths cover tracks within the reach of any reasonably fit hiker. There may be stretches, however, where those with little mountain experience should be accompanied by a guide. (See "Climbing Adventures" in Part VII for more information on guides.) These stretches may involve very steep slopes where snow can remain until late summer.

The High Routes cover altitudes from 3,937 to 10,814 feet (1,200 to 3,296 meters), where temperatures may drop very low at any time of the year. So be prepared with the proper gear. In addition to standard clothing and hiking equipment, an ice-ax or hatchet may be useful in certain areas.

AOSTA VALLEY HIGH ROUTE 1

Distance: 81 miles (130 kilometers)
Hiking time: 8 days
High point: 9.606 feet (2,928 meters)
Map: Kompass, tourist series numbers 85, 86, 87

The High Route 1 begins in Gressoney-St. Jean and extends westward to Courmayeur, covering approximately 81 miles (130 kilometers). It, and its side-paths, pass by the highest peaks from Monte Rosa to Mont Blanc. Besides these superb examples of natural architecture, this route offers incomparable examples of rustic civilization, such as the traditional constructions of the Gressoney Valley.

The rural high altitude landscape is also interesting, as in the Vallone di By in the Ollomont Valley, and the Great Saint Bernard Valley, where the traditional activities associated with pasture life are still carried out.

High Routes 1 and 2 offer many opportunities to view local wildlife as well. Some of the animals you may encounter include ibex, chamois, deer, marmot, white hare, golden eagles, black grouse and ptarmigan.

The following itinerary allows you to cover the entire High Route 1 in 8 days—without taking into account any side-trips. The daily walking time varies from 4 1/2 to 10 hours. You can also move at a slower pace, if desired and obtain lodging at centers other than those listed at the end of each day's planned route.

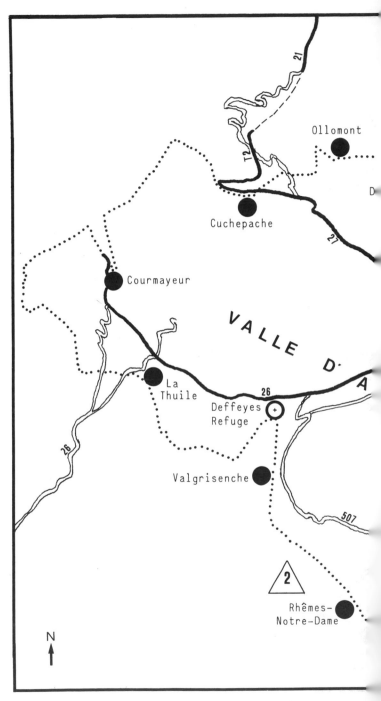

Aosta Valley High Routes 1 and 2

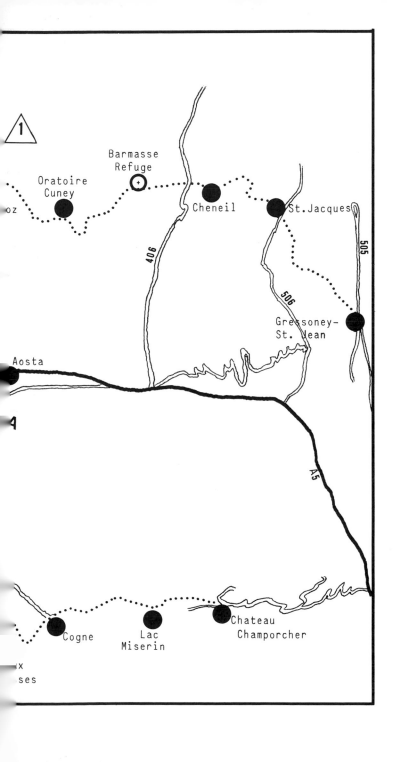

1st day: Pick-up High Route 1 at Gressoney-St. Jean (4,544 feet/1,385 meters) heading north-west—Chemonal—Colle di Pinter (9,111 feet/2,777 meters)—Crest—Rifugio Casale—St. Jacques (5,541 feet/1,689 meters).

2nd day: St. Jacques—Colle di Nana—Cheneil (6,906 feet/2,105 meters).

3rd day: Cheneil—Valtournenche—Valmartin—Rifugio Barmasse (7,116 feet/2,169 meters).

4th day: Rifugio Barmasse—Finestra d'Ersa—Grand Drayere—Fenetre-de-Tsan (8,970 feet/2,734 meters)—Le Crottes—La Servaz—Oratoire Cuney (8,701 feet/2,652 meters).

5th day: Oratoire Cuney—Col du Salvé—Col de Chaleby—Plan Piscina—Col Vessona (9,150 feet/2,789 meters)—Ardamun—La Vieille—Betenda—Close—Dzovennoz (5,167 feet/1,575 meters).

6th day: Dzovennoz—Close—Col de Breuson—Ollomont (4,449 feet/1,356 meters).

7th day: Ollomont—Alpe Champillon—Col Champillon—Creux de Bleintse—Pointier—Bezet—Eternon—Saint-Rhemy—Cuchepache (5,407 feet/1,648 meters).

8th day: Cuchepache—Merdeux-Desot—Tsa-di-Merdeux—Col Malatrà (9,606 feet/2,928 meters)—A. de Malatrà Dessus—Joet—Lavachey—Courmayeur (3,937 feet/1,200 meters).

AOSTA VALLEY HIGH ROUTE 2

Distance: 87 miles (140 kilometers)
Hiking time: 8 days
High point: 10,814 feet (3,296 meters)
Map: Kompass, tourist series numbers 85, 86, 87

The High Route 2 begins in Chateau-Champorcher and ends 8 days later—as designed here—in Courmayeur. The route covers about 87 miles (140 kilometers) with an average of 6 1/2 hours of walking each day (some days may be only 4 hours, others as much as 9).

This is a nature lover's itinerary of exceptional interest because a large part of it passes through the territory of the Gran Paradiso National Park. Here, where nature remains complete and unspoiled, it is possible to admire the grace of a running chamois or the agility of an ibex clearing difficult passes among the rocks. Or you may find yourself surrounded by a herd of male ibex as they gather towards the close of day to nibble grass at the foot of a glacier.

The ideal time to admire the flora is in July when the mountains are in full bloom. Little dots of flowers with brilliant colors, which would not be seen from down below, assume a special value here: they represent the victory of life over the austerity of the environment.

The beauty of Alpine valleys.

41

1st day: Chateau-Champorcher (4,682 feet/1,427 meters)—Chardonney—Creton—Dondena—Lac Miserin (8,458 feet/2,578 meters).

2nd day: Lac Miserin—Lac Ner—Fenetre de Champorcher (9,272 feet/2,826 meters)—Peradza—Bruillot—P. Bardoney—Goilles—Lillaz—Cogne (5,069 feet/1,545 meters).

3rd day: Cocne—Valnontey—Rifugio V. Sella—Col Lauson (10,814 feet/3,296 meters)—Livionaz-Desot—Eaux Rousses (5,466 feet/1,666 meters).

4th day: Eaux Rousses—Orvieille—Lac Djouan—Col de l'Entrelor (9,849 feet/3,002 meters)—Plan di Feye—Entrelor—Rhêmes-Notre-Dame (5,653 feet/1,723 meters).

5th day: Rhêmes-Notre-Dame—Torrent—Col Fenetre—Epee-di-Plontains—Praz-Londzet—Valgrisenche (5,460 feet/1,664 meters).

6th day: Valgrisenche—Revers—Planaval—Baraques du Fond—Pas de Planaval (9,875 feet/3,010 meters)—it is often impossible to get through the Planaval pass without an ice-ax, crampons and rope)—Rifugio Deffeyes (8,202 feet/2,500 meters).

7th day: Rifugio Deffeyes—Alpade du Ruto—Lac du Glacier—2nd Cascade—La Joux—La Thuile (4,728 feet/1,441 meters).

8th day: La Thuile—Pont-Serrand—Porassey—A. Chavannes-Dessus—Col des Chavannes—Rifugio Elisabetta—Courmayeur (3,937 feet/1,200 meters).

CHIAVENNA VALLEY ROUTE

Distance: 34 miles (55 kilometers)
Hiking time: 6 days
High point: 9,852 feet (3,003 meters)
Map: Kompass tourist series, "Sentieri e Rifugi"

The Val Chiavenna is formed by 3 major valleys and several minor ones. The 3 principle valleys are: the Bassa Val Chiavenna that climbs from Lake Como to the north along the Mera River; the Val Bregaglia that leads from Chiavenna to the Swiss border at Castasegna and from there to the Maioja-Engadina Pass; and the Val San Giacomo which climbs towards the Spiuga Pass.

Since prehistoric times the Val Chiavenna has provided a connection between the Po River Basin and the Valley of Reno. It has seen a constant stream of soldiers, merchants, religious refugees, politicians and tourists passing through.

Of particular interest to walkers are the glacial erosion in the Val Chiavenna region, and the breathtaking summits, lakes and waterfalls. The Acqua Fragia Falls and the Pianazzo Falls, which crash down more than 590 feet (180 meters) are among the most famous.

Chiavenna, the chief town of the valley, conserves much of its medieval appearance and its characteristic "crotti"— ancient natural cellars.

Leaving from Campodolcino, the route begins with a climb to the Angeloga Alp, where you'll find a lake of the same name. On its banks the Chiavenna shelter stands in a tranquil oasis under the walls of the "Pizzo Stella" (Star Peak) and the "Pizzo Groppara" (Groppara Peak). These peaks must be climbed in order to reach the Motta Alp and the hills of the Andossi, as far as the shelter Stuetta in the high Spluga Valley. From here you'll make your way to the "Pizzo Ferre" glaciers and the highest point along the route—9,852 feet/3,003 meters—at the summit of Val Loga. At this point, the trail descends along the Cardinello Path, which takes you to Isola, the lowest point of the Val San Giacomo. From here you'll return to Campodolcino where the venture began.

The average daily walking time is 5 hours.

1st day: From Campodolcino (3,609 feet/1,100 meters)— Fraciscio—Angeloga Alp— Chiavenna Refuge (6,690 feet/2,039 meters).

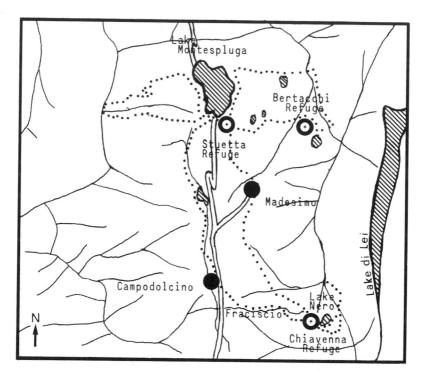

Chiavenna Valley Route

2nd day: Chiavenna Refuge—Angeloga Pass—Pizzo Groppara (9,672 feet/2,948 meters)—Angeloga Pass—Lake Nero—Chiavenna Refuge.

3rd day: Chiavenna Refuge—Motta Alp—Madesimo—Andossi—Stuetta Refuge (6,102 feet/1,860 meters).

4th day: Stuetta Refuge—Lake Nero Pass (8,428 feet/ 2,569 meters)—Pizzo Spadolazzo (8,924 feet/2,720 meters)—Emet Pass—Bertacchi Refuge (7,205 feet/2,196 meters)—Lake Andossi—Stuetta Refuge.

5th day: Stuetta Refuge—Lake Montespluga—Val Loga (9,852 feet/3,003 meters)— Val Sghisarolo—Stuetta Refuge.

6th day: Stuetta Refuge—Cardinello Path—Mottalerra—Isola—Campodolcino.

VALMASINO ROUTE

Distance: 37 miles (60 kilometers)
Hiking time: 5 days
High point: 12,067 feet (3,678 meters)
Map: Kompass, tourist series, "Sentieri e Rifugi"

In a natural, absolutely integral and uncontaminated environment, the Valmasino offers magnificent excursions and ascents. Bordered to the north by Switzerland, Valmasino has not had the flow of traffic through history that other areas have. As a result, it maintains an individuality unlike most alpine regions.

Several lateral valleys detach themselves from the principal furrow of the Valmasino: the valley of Preda Rossa, the Val di Mello, the valley of the Bagni and the Val Porcellizzo Mary are but a few. Many famous summits form the scenery of Valmasino, including the Disgrazia, the Sissone, the Pizzi del Ferro, the Cengalo and the Badile.

There are also numerous shelters which are reached only by foot, most entailing a minimum of 2 hours climbing. In addition to these shelters, the valley offers permanent bivouacs, such as Molteni-Valsecchi, Manzi, Odello-Grandori and Ronconi.

Along the route one finds mountain people who, with age-old patience, have made terraces on steep slopes for vineyards and built homes from which herds are led to high pastures during the summer months.

The peculiar conformation of the Valmasino and of the lateral valleys that towards the north open into spacious meadows, give rise to considerable changes of temperature and permit a wide variety of vegetation to grow: from beeches to red and white fir trees, to rhododendron and varied prairie and herbaceous species.

The Valmasino Route begins and ends in the village of Filorera, covering approximately 37 miles (60 kilometers). As outlined, the route can be easily covered in 5 days with an average walking time per day of 6 hours.

1st day: Beginning in the village of Filorera, climb the head of the valley of Oro up to the Rifugio Omio (6,890 feet/ 2,100 meters)—Along the route, one encounters a number of hamlets and mountain pastures.

2nd day: Rifugio Omio—Pizzi dell'Oro—Rifugio Giannetti (8,314 feet/2,534 meters).

3rd day: Rifugio Giannetti—Camerozzo Pass (8,924 feet/ 2,720 meters)—Qualido Pass (8,684 feet/2,647 meters)—Rifugio Allievi (7,837 feet/2,389 meters).

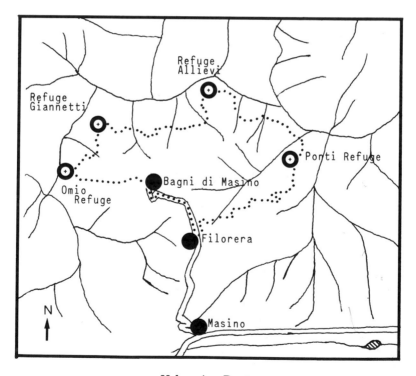

Valmasino Route

46

4th day: Rifugio Allievi—Val Torrone Pass—Cameraccio Pass—Mount Disgrazia (12,067 feet/3,678 meters)—Ponti Hut (8,396 feet/2,559 meters).

5th day: Ponti Hut—Sasso Bisolo Valley—Filorera.

CAMONICA VALLEY-CAMUNNI ROUTE

Distance: 46 miles (74 kilometers)
Hiking time: 5 days
High point: 7,608 feet (2,319 meters)
Map: Kompass, tourist series, "Sentieri e Rifugi"

The setting of the Camunni civilization is a mountainous zone where at least a strip of snow is always visible, even in the hottest of summers. It is a world of forest and meadows where under Badile Camuno Peak and Mount Concarena an ancient civilization of 8,000 years ago has left evidence of itself sculptured in the rock.

With 170,000 engravings dating from 6,000 BC to the Roman conquest in 16 BC, it is the most complete and significant artistic and cultural patrimony left to us from prehistory. There are several hundred engraved rocks upon which the ancient Camunni civilization represented the most significant aspects of their society (ploughing, hunting, religious rites, symbology, myths, family and sexual life, and war.).

The Camonica Valley unwinds from Lake Iseo, at the Tonale Pass, between two splendid mountain chains covered by luxuriant forests of alders, chestnuts, birches, pines, firs and larches. On the heights one finds ample pastures where the herds spend the summer. (An excellent cheese is obtained here.) At the foot of the mountain or scattered halfway up its side are numerous small towns that guard ancient traditions in the rustic architecture, in handicrafts such as weaving with centuries-old looms or the manufacturing of baskets by hand.

The Camonica Valley-Camunni Route begins and ends in Edolo, a picturesque mountain village. The trail is approximately 46 miles (74 kilometers) and can be easily walked in 5 days, assuming no side-trips are taken. The following itinerary allows for 5 to 6 hours of walking each day.

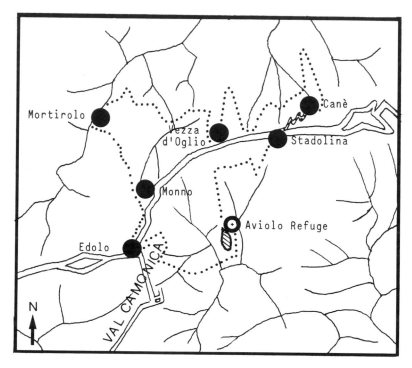

Camonica Valley-Camunni Route

1st day: Edolo (2,346 feet/715 meters)—Monno—Mortirolo (5,413 feet/1,650 meters).

2nd day: Mortirolo—Grom Valley—Col di Val Bighera (6,778 feet/2,066 meters)— Val Bighera—Val Grande—Vezza d'Oglio.

3rd day: Vezza d'Oglio—Vione—Val di Canè—Canè.

4th day: Canè—Stadolina (this section of the route may be covered by walking the main road from one town to the other, or by means of a local bus)—Val di Vallaro (4,747 feet/1,447 meters)—Prà del Mulo—(5,000 feet/1,524 meters)—Alla Cascata shelter—Rifugio Aviolo (6,332 feet/1,930 meters).

5th day: Rifugio Aviolo—Gallinera Pass (7,608 feet/2,319 meters)—Val Gallinera—Stain Malga—Edolo.

LIVIGNO TRAIL

Distance: 38 miles (60 kilometers)
Hiking time: 5 days
High point: 9,596 feet (2,925 meters)
Map: Kompass, tourist series, "Sentieri e Rifugi"

At the center of the Rhaetian Alps, between the Stelvio and the Bernina mountains, at 5,958 feet (1,816 meters) above sea level, the valley of Livigno opens up. This valley, with its north-south bearing and typical "U" shape, is irrigated along its whole length by the Spol torrent, a tributary of the Inn and of the Danube. The zone is rich in pastureland.

The bottom of the valley is crossed by a road along which the houses that constitute Livigno form a line 5 miles (8 kilometers) long; Livigno is a characteristic "road center."

Along the sides of the valley one can see old wooden houses isolated among the meadows, stables, hay-lofts and fountains. These are what remain of the time when a proper town-structure did not exist, so much as a string of inhabited centers often linked only by kinship, property or common-use relations.

The Livigno Valley is crossed by the Stelvio National Park and borders on the Engadina National Park. For this reason it is rich in environmental beauty: forests, pastures, a variety of flora, torrents and waterfalls. Stupendous alpine lakes and glaciers encircle the charming valley.

Animals roam freely in this zone: steinbock, chamois, deer, marmot and even the eagle are familiar in the valley.

June through October is the best time to trek in this area. As outlined below, the entire route can be covered in 5 days, with an average of 6 hours walking each day.

1st day: From Livigno, a trip to Mount Motta (8,911 feet/ 2,716 meters) in the Stelvio National Park—Return to Livigno.

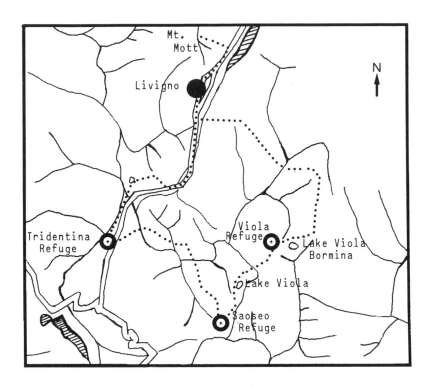

Livigno Trail

2nd day: Livigno—Lago del Monte (Mountain Lake)—La Breva (9,281 feet/2,829 meters)—Tridentina Rifugio (7,595 feet/2,315 meters).

3rd day: Tridentina Rifugio—Orsera Pass (9,596 feet/2,925 meters)—Mera Pass (8,776 feet/2,675 meters)—Saoseo Rifugio (6,519 feet/1,987 meters) in Swiss territory.

4th day: Saoseo Rifugio—Viola Lake—Viola Pass (7,979 feet/ 2,432 meters)—Viola Rifugio (7,726 feet/2,355 meters).

The Dolomite mountain range.

5th day: Viola Rifugio—Viola Bormina Lake—Minestra Valley—Colle delle Mine (9,189 feet/2,801 meters)—Mine Valley—Livigno.

STELVIO TREK

Distance: 37 miles (60 kilometers)
Hiking time: 6 days
High point: 9,265 feet (2,824 meters)
Map: Kompass, tourist series, "Sentieri e Rifugi"

This trek takes you through the valleys of Bormio's outskirts, in a national park that represents a true reservoir of wildlife, greenery, peace and ecological equilibrium. This is one of the few protected and uncontaminated areas of the Alps. Along this route there will be time to admire the beauty.

The Bormio region has a long history. Already famous at the time of the Romans for its thermal water, it was later the capital of an ancient earldom and an important cultural center.

The mountains, the towers, churches, ancient buildings and hospitality that one encounters in those valleys that formed the "Magnifica Terra" (The Magnificent Land) all echo with events of the past.

The Stelvio Route, which begins in Arnoga (8.7 miles/14 kilometers by bus from Bormio) can be covered in 6 days, with an average of 5 hours walking each day. This particular trek can best be enjoyed during the months of May through October.

1st day: Arnoga—Malga Verva (6,398 feet/1,950 meters)—Verva Pass (7,549 feet/2,301 meters)—Eita (5,587 feet/1,703 meters), evening in local hut.

2nd day: Eita—Lakes of Tres (7,172 feet/2,186 meters)—Lake Negro (8,399 feet/2,560 meters)—Dosdè Pass (9,265 feet/2,824 meters)—Dosdè Rifugio.

3rd day: Dosdè Rifugio—Dosdè Alp (6,985 feet/2,129 meters)—Lake of Val Viola (7,438 feet/2,267 meters)—Viola Rifugio (7,438 feet/2,267 meters).

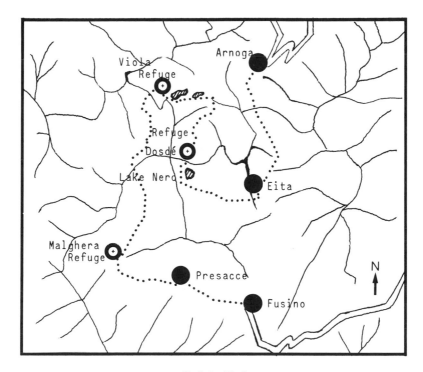

Stelvio Trek

4th day: Viola Rifugio—Viola Pass (7,979 feet/2,432 meters)—Sacco Pass (8,957 feet/2,730 meters)—Malghera Rifugio (6,443 feet/1,964 meters).

5th day: Malghera Rifugio—West Val Grosina—Presacce (4,757 feet/1,450 meters), evening in local hut.

6th day: Presacce—Fusino. Return, via bus, to Bormio (14.3 miles/23 kilometers).

ORTLES-CEVEDALE TRAIL

Distance: 45 miles (72 kilometers)
Hiking time: 6 days

High point: 11,676 feet (3,559 meters)
Map: Kompass, tourist series, "Sentieri e Rifugi"

Valfurva, the heart of the Stelvio National Park is bordered by an ample chain of mountains, forming a vast semi-circle. The Cevedale is the central point of the entire mountain arc. This is the departing point of the "Tredici Cime" (The Thirteen Summits) that reach the characteristic pyramidic structure of the Tresero with a ridge 22 miles (35 kilometers) long, at elevations over 10,499 feet (3,200 meters).

The valley offers a varied environment: coniferous trees, red firs, alders and typically alpine landscapes such as marshy plants close to small lakes and alpine tundra on the snowiest slopes. On the right slope, the splendid forests often come down as far as the Frodolfo torrent that runs throughout the valley. In the underbrush there is a variety of mosses and mushrooms.

The old mule-track leading to the pass still retains many traces of the ancient Venetian paving made up of large stones. It was upgraded during World War I to permit the conveyance of heavy ordnance.

The trail, as outlined, can easily be covered in 6 days, each day consisting of an average of 5 hours walking. The best time of the year to venture along the Ortles-Cevedale Trail is June through September. The route begins at St. Caterina Valfurva and ends in Gavia Pass.

1st day: St. Caterina Valfurva (5,702 feet/1,738 meters)—Glacier of the Forni–Rifugio Branca.

2nd day: Rifugio Branca—Rifugio Casati (10,715 feet/3.266 meters)—Rifugo Pizzini.

3rd day: Rifugio Pizzini—5th Alpini Path to Zebrù Pass—Rifugio 5th Alpini.

4th day: Rifugio 5th Alpini—a visit to the dominating glaciers—Zebrù Valley—St. Antonio Valfurva.

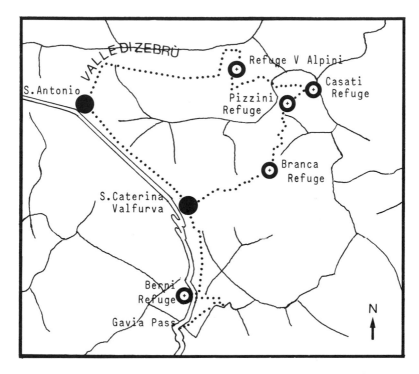

Ortles-Cevedale Trail

5th day: St. Antonio Valfurva—St. Caterina—Pian della Marmotte—(Roman Path) Rifugio Berni.

6th day: Rifugio Berni—Dosegù Valley—Vall'Umbrina (11,676 feet/3,559 meters)—Gavia Pass (8,589 feet/2,618 meters).

DOLOMITES HIGH ROUTE 1

Distance: 37 miles (60 kilometers)
Hiking time: 11 days
High point: 9,350 feet (2,850 meters)
Map: Zone Turistiche d'Italia, Touring Club Italiano

The Dolomites High Route 1 crosses the very heart of the Dolomite Mountain Range from north to south: from the Pusteria to the edge of the Veneto Plain, passing from the Dolomites of Brajes to Cortina d'Ampezzo, the Zoldano, the Agordino to Belluno.

There is an immense variety in natural scenery and human contacts to be enjoyed at the leisurely speed of an alpine walker.

The High Route makes use of paths within the capacities of any walker, requiring a minimum of equipment but some experience of mountains. Numerous deviations and recommended climbs will be found along the main route which, while not presenting real rock climbing difficulties, do require prudence and a steady head.

It is advisable to undertake the trip after the snow has melted (when the refuges are open)—not earlier than the end of June. September is the best month, because of the settled weather and the beauty of the landscape. October, too, is good

Ground squirrels can be seen along many mountain trails.

56

if weather conditions are favorable. Keep in mind, however, that refuges begin to close by September 15th.

The route is well posted, with alpine trail markers. Walkers should have no problems finding their way. As designed, the following daily itineraries allow for an average of 5 to 9 hours of walking. But you need not stick to these specific stops. In fact, many prefer to simply head out for the day and stop at the nearest refuge whenever they feel tired.

From the Lake of Brajes to Belluno requires about 11 days, but 14 are recommended, keeping in mind that some extra days may be needed for rest, optional diversions, or because of bad weather. Well-trained walkers on the other hand have accomplished the whole journey in 7 or 8 days.

An excellent booklet on the "High Route of the Dolomites N.1" is available, in English, from the Ente Provinciale per il Turismo, via Psaro 21, 32100 Belluno, Italy. The booklet provides detailed descriptions of the route as well as several side trips and alternative activities for the climber.

1st day: Lake of Brajes—Rifugio Biella (7,546 feet/2,300 meters)—Rifugio Sennes (6,975 feet/2,126 meters)—Rifugio Fodara Vedla—Rifugio Pederù (5,079 feet/1,548 meters)—Val di Rudo—Pices Fanes Valley—Rifugio Fanes (6,699 feet/2,042 meters) and Rifugio Varella (6,758 feet/2,060 meters).

2nd day: Rifugio Fanes (or Varella)—Passo Limo (7,126 feet/2,172 meters)—Malga (mountain farm) Fanes Grande—Steep climb through the Vallon Bianco to the Forcella Casale (9,350 feet/2,850 meters)—Monte Cavallo (7,192 feet/2,192 meters)—Steep descent in the Val Travenanzes—Now the steep rocky slope of the Masarè must be climbed by the exposed "iron ladder" on the mass of the Tofane, in order to reach the stony bowl between the Tre Tofane (The Masarè) and the Rifugio Cantone (8,350 feet/2,434 meters).

3rd day: Rifugio Cantone—Rifugio Dibona—"Sote Cordes" pathway—Tofana di Roces—Forcella Bos—Rifugio Cinque Torri (7,011 feet/2,137 meters)—Rifugio Nuvolau (8,448 feet/2,575 meters).

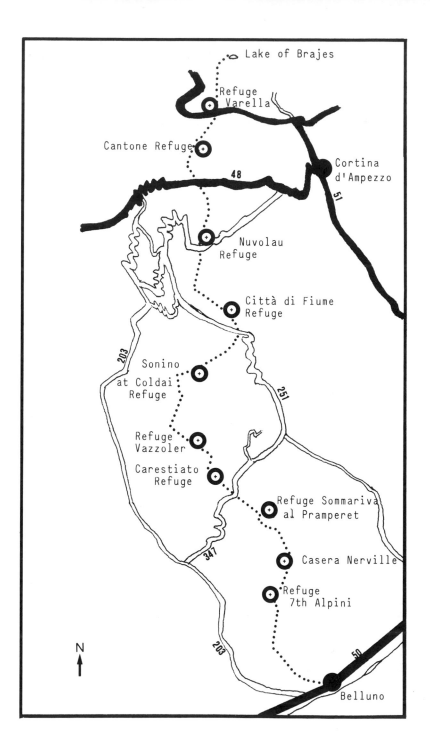

Lake of Brajes

Refuge
Varella

Cantone Refuge

Cortina
d'Ampezzo

48

51

Nuvolau
Refuge

Città di Fiume
Refuge

203

Sonino
at Coldai
Refuge

251

Refuge
Vazzoler

Carestiato
Refuge

Refuge Sommariva
al Pramperet

347

Casera Nerville

Refuge
7th Alpini

203

50

N

Belluno

4th day: Rifugio Nuvolau—Passo Giau (7,336 feet/2,236 meters)—Forcella Nuvolau—Forcella Giau (7,785 feet/2,373 meters)—Forcella Ambrizzola (7,470 feet/2,277 meters)—Becco del Mezzodi—Forcella Col Duro (7,523 feet/2,293 meters)—down to Col Roan (6,818 feet/2,078 meters—Pass under the west flank of Ponta Puina—Rifugio Città di Fiume (6,289 feet/1,917 meters).

5th day: Rifugio Città di Fiume—Triol dei Cavai—Col de le Creppe Cavaliere (6,262 feet/1,909 meters)—Rifugio Venezia/De Luca—Val di Zoldo—Casera Pioda (6,286 feet/1,916 meters)—Rifugio Sonino at Coldai (7,005 feet/2,135 meters).

6th day: Rifugio Sonino at Coldai—Rifugio Tissi—Val Civetta—Rifugio Vazzoler (5,748 feet/1,752 meters).

7th day: Rifugio Vazzoler—Val Corpassa—Mount Moiazze—Col de l'Ors (5,905 feet/1,800 meters)—Forcella del Camp (6,339 feet/1,932 meters)—Rifugio Carestiato (6,037 feet/1,840 meters).

8th day: Rifugio Carestiato—Passo Duran (5,266 feet/1,605 meters)— Agordo/Zoldo road (347)—Ponte di Caleda (5,052 feet/1,540 meters)—Pick up route immediately after and go up to Forcella Dagarei (5,315 feet/1,620 meters)—Col Pan d'Orso (5,823 feet/1,775 meters)—Forcella Moschesin (6,365 feet/1,940 meters)—Pra della Vedova by way of the "Sentiero delle Balanzole"—Rifugio Sommariva al Pramperet (6,152 feet/1,875 meters).

9th day: Rifugio Sommariva al Pramperet—Portela del Piazadel (6,880 feet/2,097 meters)—Forcella Sud dei Van de Città (7,858 feet/2,395 meters)—Casera Pian de Fontana (5,354 feet/1,632 meters)—Forcella La Varetta (5,590 feet/1,704 meters)—Casera Nerville (5,384 feet/1,641 meters).

Dolomites High Route 1

10th day: Casera Nerville—Climb the north ravine between Pelf and Schiara mountains—Forcella del Marmol (7,421 feet/2,262 meters)—Bivouac of the Marmol—"Iron ladder of the Marmol"—Rifugio 7th Alpini (4,888 feet/1,490 meters).

11th day: Rifugio 7th Alpini—Via mule track through the Val d'Ardo—Case Bortot (2,320 feet/707 meters)—Road to Belluno.

Gran Paradiso National Park Hikes

Italy's first National Park, the Gran Paradiso, was established in 1922 between the Valley of Aosta and Piedmont regions, in an environment of beautiful valleys that open to the south from the river Dora Baltea. This is on the northernmost spurs of Canavese, the highest entirely Italian mountain range. The territory of the park covers 172,900 acres, three-fifths of which is in the Valley of Aosta. It is predominantly mountainous and is almost entirely above 4,921 feet (1,500 meters), reaching 13,323 feet (4,061 meters) at the Gran Paradiso peak.

Five main valleys, each one distinct from the others, cross the park: three of them in the Valley of Aosta (the Valley of Rhemes, the Valsavarenche and the Valley of Cogne) and the other two (Orco and Soana) on the Canavese side of the park. All these valleys are easily accessible. On the southern side deep and narrow valleys slope steeply into the Orco Valley, while in the much larger territory of the Valley of Aosta, valleys are longer and wider.

Among the birds in the highest zones are the snow finch, the alpine accentor, the wall creeper, the rock partridge, the alpine chough and the ptarmigan. Principal birds living in the conifer woods are the black grouse, the hazel hen, the black woodpecker, the nutcracker and other noctural birds of prey. In the same altitudes live citril finches peculiar to the mountains of Western Europe.

In the mountains of the park, and to some extent throughout the Alps, there also appear birds which are not exclusive to mountain zones: crows, black redstart, alpine swift, crag martin and wheatear. The most imposing bird of the park is the golden eagle which, although not a typical mountain bird, lives almost exclusively in the mountains of this region.

The great reputation of the park stems from its mammals. Ibex and chamois are the largest. During the summer months, marmot enliven the mountain pastures. In the higher altitudes snow vole are often found. In addition to many insectivores, bats and tiny rodents, Gran Paradiso maintains a population of red fox, stoat, weasel, beech marten, pine marten and badger.

Unfortunately, even here some species have declined in recent years due to human intrusion. Bearded vultures, lynx and wild cat were abundant here during the last century. Today these species have disappeared.

Sixty percent of the park is covered by forests of larch and spruce. There are also many rare alpine plant species, starting at about the 2,625 feet (800 meters) level.

The beauty of nature in the Aosta Valley.

Getting to the Gran Paradiso National Park

Situated near the Little and Great St. Bernard Passes (open only in the summer), the park is easily accessible by several means of transportation. Aosta, which can be reached by train or by car from Milan (106 miles/170 kilometers) or from Turin (70 miles/113 kilometers), lies 30 minutes by car from the chief centers of the Gran Paradiso. By driving along the "superstrada" of Mont Blanc tunnel, a short distance beyond Aosta, you join the state road to Cogne and the park. From Villeneuve, roads lead off to the valleys of Rhemes and Valsavarenche. From Turin all the principal centers of the Canavese valleys are accessible within 2 hours' drive. Bus service is also available, except for winter months in the Valsavarenche and the Valley of Rhemes.

Obtaining Information

Before venturing to the Gran Paradiso National Park, you might want to write for free information from one or more of the following agencies.

Head Office and Management of the Gran Paradiso National Park: Via della Rocca 47, 10123 Torino, Italy; tel: (011) 871–187.

Administrative Office of the Gran Paradiso National Park: Via Losanna 5, 11100 Aosta, Italy; tel: (0165) 44–126.

Provincial Tourist Office: Piazza C.L.N. 228, 10121 Torino, Italy.

The Most Interesting Excursions

The park satisfies the visitor's curiosity in every season: winter is suitable for ski trips while summer is the best time for walks and excursions. You can visit the park almost entirely on foot; a complex network of paths and mule-tracks, rationally marked out, winds for 292 miles (470 kilometers) through the most interesting sections. Of particular interest are the tracks half-way up the mountains, between 6,561 and 9,900 feet (2,000 and 2,600 meters).

The following itineraries have been established by the Italian Alpine Club and are suggested for anyone interested in hiking for a single day. Routes can also be combined for those desiring longer excursions.

RHÊMES-NOTRE-DAME ROUTE (trails 303, 307, 315, 302)

Distance: 6.2 miles (10 kilometers)
Hiking time: 3.5 hours
High point: 7,529 feet (2,295 meters)

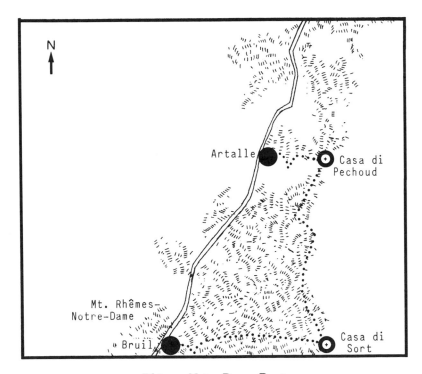

Rhêmes-Notre-Dame Route

Map: Parco Nazionale del Gran Paradiso, Touring Club
Italiano

This route begins on the north-west edge of the park, from the
information center dedicated to Renzo Videsott in the town of
Bruil, at the foot of the Rhêmes-Notre-Dame mountain. Here,
you'll find trail 303 running south through the forest. Following this for about 30 minutes, you eventually turn and head
north-east, leaving route 303 and picking up route 307. Continue along 307, always through heavy wooded lands until, at
7,529 feet (2,295 meters), you exit the forests at the Casa di
Sort, a shelter for park guards. This is a glacier zone as you
will see. Not far from the shelter to the north is another trail
(number 315) which will lead you once again into the forest.
Forty-five minutes along the trail, you will reach a beautiful
lookout point at the foot of the Chaussettaz Mountain (7,188
feet/2,191 meters). The trail branches off here, making a "Y".
Continue along trail 315 to the right. In a short while this will
take you out of the woods across an open mountain zone and
again into the woods. Soon you will come into an opening and
the Casa di Pechoud, another park shelter, to the north. Here
you change routes again, picking up number 302 which runs
west. Another 45 minutes of forest walking and you will come
to the town of Artalle, the end of the Rhêmes-Notre-Dame
Route.

VALSAVARENCHE WAY (trails 303, 210, 211, 207)

Distance: 11 miles (18 kilometers)
Hiking time: 8 hours
High point: 11,866 feet (3,116 meters)
Map: Parco Nazionale del Gran Paradiso, Touring Club
Italiano

Beginning in Bruil, at the foot of Mount Rhêmes-Notre-Dame,
take trail 303 south from the park information center. Shortly,
trail 307 branches off to your left. Remain on 303. There are
several very good panoramas along this route, including one
which overlooks Mount di Entrelor, visible as you exit the

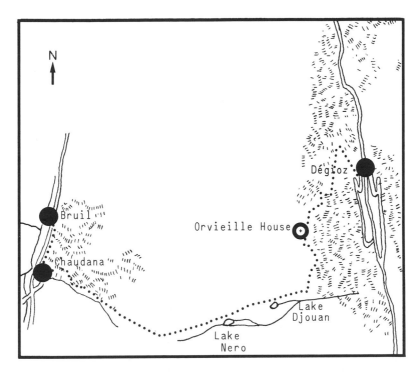

Valsavarenche Way

woods and head for the Plain of Feyes (7,884 feet/2,403 meters). From here, continue along route 303 to the Colle di Entrelor and Lake Nero. In poor weather this section of the trail can be hazardous as it rises along the mountain to 11,866 feet (3,116 meters). From Lake Nero, follow trail 210 past Lake Djouan and pick up route 211 heading north past Mount Djouan. At 8,579 feet (2,615 meters) you'll encounter the Orvieille House, a shelter for park rangers. At this point, take trail 207 which winds through the forest and eventually ends in the village of Dégioz.

EAU ROUSSE ROUTE (trail 206)

Distance: 4.3 miles (7 kilometers)
Hiking time: 5.5 hours

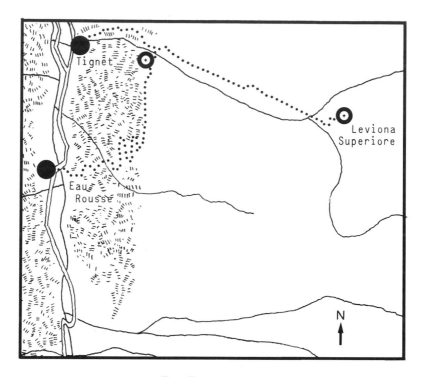

Eau Rousse Route

High point: 8,688 feet (2,648 meters)
Map: Parco Nazionale del Gran Paradiso, Touring Club
Italiano

The Eau Rousse route follows trail 206 from the village of
Tignet, where you can find food and lodging at a local refuge.
The route runs along the Leviona River, taking the eastern
branch of the trail (to the left at the lookout point) to Leviona
Superiore (8,688 feet/2,648 meters). You then return along the
route to the lookout point. Here you'll pick up the western
branch of 206, walk parallel to the forest, finally entering it
and pursuing a zig-zag route into the town of Eau Rousse.

NOASCA—GRAN PIANO (trail 548)

Distance: 3.7 miles (6 kilometers)
Hiking time: 5 hours
High point: 7,290 feet (2,222 meters)
Map: Parco Nazionale del Gran Paradiso, Touring Club
Italiano

This route takes you from the town of Noasca, along the western side of Mount Castell through the Valley of Ciamosseretto. From Noasca take trail 548 up to Sassa, a tiny mountain village. Continue along the route into the woods. In about 20 minutes trail 548 forks. You remain on the uphill route to the left. This will lead you through the woods and, eventually, into

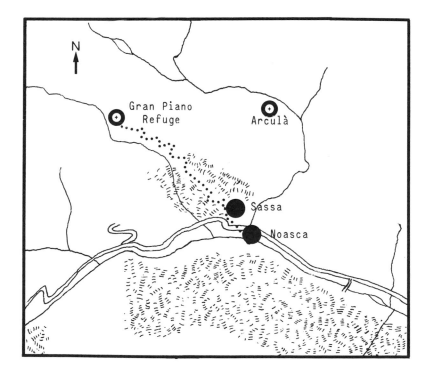

Noasca-Gran Piano

an open meadow. There is a cascade to your left which is worth seeing. After visiting the cascade, continue the uphill walk to the park shelter at 7,290 feet (2,222 meters). The panorama here is breathtaking. You return to Noasca along the same route.

VALNONTEY ROUTE (trail 105, 104)

Distance: 2.5 miles (4 kilometers)
Hiking time: 4 hours
High point: 7,628 feet (2,325 meters)
Map: Parco Nazionale del Gran Paradiso, Touring Club Italiano

From Valnontey's Gran Paradiso Camp Ground head south along the 105/104 trail, which runs parallel to the Valnontey

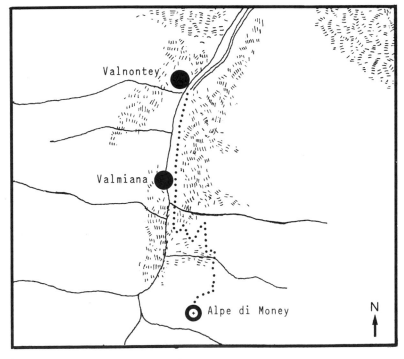

Valnontey Route

River. Soon you'll pass through the village of Valmiana and into the woods. After roughly 20 minutes of walking, the trail forks, becoming 105 (to the right) and 104 (to the left). Take 104 uphill into the forest. There are several panoramic points along the remainder of the route, which eventually leads you to the Alpe di Money lookout point and park shelter at 7,628 feet (2,325 meters). You return via the same route.

LILLAZ TRAIL (trail 102)

Distance: 5.9 miles (9.5 kilometers)
Hiking time: 4.3 hours
High point: 7,723 feet (2,354 meters)
Map: Parco Nazionale del Gran Paradiso, Touring Club Italiano

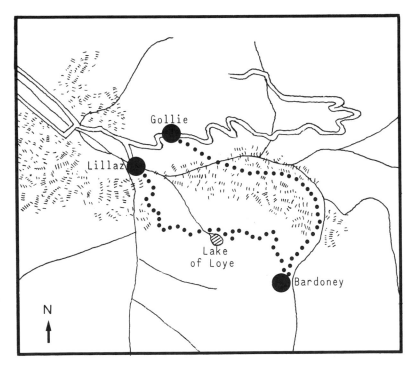

Lillaz Trail

The Lillaz trail begins in the mountain village of Lillaz, where camping facilities are available. From the town, head southeast on trail 102 to the alpine Lake of Loye, at 7,723 feet (2,354 meters). This is beautiful country, with superb panoramic views. Continue along the trail, east, to the foot of the Testa Goilles peak where you turn south to Bardoney. From here, trail 102 goes north-east around Testa Goilles, eventually going into the woods as it turns and heads north-west. At 6,083 feet (1,854 meters) you will pass through the village of Gollie. Shortly thereafter, you'll find the Cascade of Lillaz on your left. From here it is a short walk to Lillaz.

PIAMPRATO HIKE (trail 630)

Distance: 5.9 miles (9.5 kilometers)

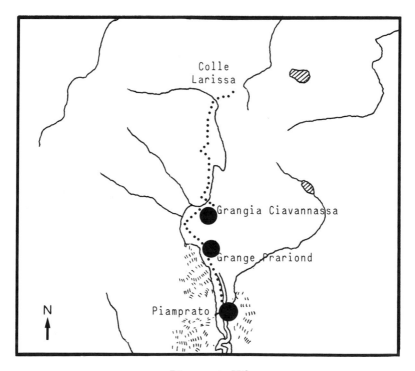

Piamprato Hike

Hiking time: 5 hours
High point: 8,478 feet (2,584 meters)
Map: Parco Nazionale del Gran Paradiso, Touring Club
Italiano

This is a relatively straight route running north from the village of Piamprato. The trail, 630, starts on the north side of town and parallels the River Piamprato, through open meadows. You'll pass the villages of Grange Prariond and Grangia Ciavannassa, before crossing the river and heading due north. The trail leads past Grangia La Reale to the lookout point at Colle Larissa on the park's border (8,478 feet/2,584 meters). The return trip is along the same route (630).

VALLEY OF FORZO (trail 608)

Distance: 6.8 miles (11 kilometers)
Hiking time: 5 hours
High point: 7,057 feet (2,151 meters)
Map: Parco Nazionale del Gran Paradiso, Touring Club
Italiano

From Molino di Forzo, take trail 608 uphill to Tressi and north through the Valley of Forzo. The route runs parallel to the Torrente Forzo, with a number of picturesque cascades along the way. At this point you are walking through forest. Once you have reached Boschietto, an ancient settlement, leave the main trail and head north up the Gran Giavina mountain to the shelter at 7,057 feet (2,151 meters). After visiting the peak, descend the same route and turn right onto trail 608, continuing along a north-western course. Walking parallel to the woods, you travel in open meadows, passing through the villages of Boschiettiera and Gran Pian Lavina before getting to the lookout point at Costa. From here you'll have to backtrack on trail 608 for the return trip.

Stelvio National Park

Founded in 1935, the Stelvio National Park encompasses

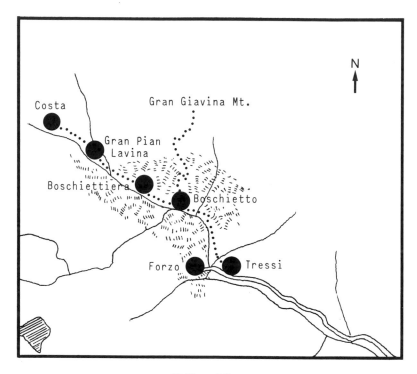

Valley of Forzo

3,383,900 acres of land in the central Alps of northern Italy. The park ranges from 3,280 to 13,123 feet (1,000 to 4,000 meters) above sea level and takes in mountains, high meadows, nearly 100 active glaciers, rock formations and forests.

Stelvio is rich with rare alpine flora. Forests are made up chiefly of conifers such as larch, spruce, cembrain pine, Scotch pine and Swiss mountain pine.

Fauna within the park includes the golden eagle (symbol of the Stelvio Park), marmot, stoat, cock of the woods and black grouse among others. The most important large mammals are the red and roe deer. The ibex was recently reintroduced from the neighboring Swiss Park of Engadine.

In the park zone, it is forbidden to: hunt and fish; kill, injure or capture animals; start fires and camp in areas other than those designated for such activities; litter; remove or damage

Bull elk in Stelvio National Park.

plants; extract minerals; let dogs run free; take photographs for commercial sale; and leave designated hiking trails.

Administering the park is the State Agency of Forests, Bureau of Bormio, 23032 Italy. Maps and general information about the park can be obtained from this organization or by writing the Regional Tourist Office of Trentino Alto Adige (address in Appendix C).

Getting to the Stelvio National Park

The Stelvio National Park is close to the regions of Lombardy, Trentino and Alto Adige.

From Milan, Highways 36 and 38 will take you to the park. You can also take a train, though some connections will have to be made. From Bergamo, take Highway 42 through the town of Ponte di Legno and into the park. Trento is 42 miles (68 kilometers) from Stelvio via Highway 43. Bolzano is a short distance from the park using Highway 38, or local trains.

A Note on Trail Markings

Several of the routes discussed in the following pages are designated by trail numbers of the Italian Alpine Club as well as park itinerary numbers. In most cases, both numbers are clearly indicated so it is easy to follow your selected route. You should, however, be aware that such numbers do overlap from one organization to another. The trail numbers used in this book are those of the Italian Alpine Club, unless otherwise indicated.

VAL ZEBRÙ TRAIL (trail 10)

Distance: 10 miles (16 kilometers)
Hiking time: 9 hours
High point: 9,442 feet (2,878 meters)
Map: Parco Nazionale dello Stelvio, Touring Club Italiano

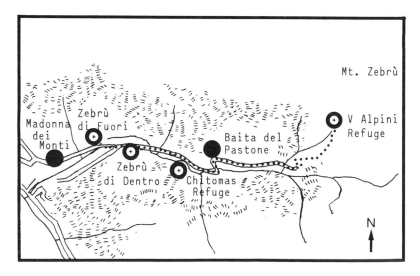

Val Zebrù Trail

The Val Zebrù trail, like most of the routes in the Stelvio Park, is best walked in July, August and September, when the snow has melted and mountain flora is the most colorful. At the bridge of Tre Croci, outside the village of Madonna dei Monti, you can leave your auto, if driving, and pick up alpine trail 10, heading north-east. There are several locations for panoramic views before you cross the River Zebrù at 5,715 feet (1,742 meters) and make your way to the Zebrù di Fuori Refuge. Continuing, you pass the Zebrù di Dentro Refuge to the right and, further along, the Chitomas Refuge. Halfway through the walk, you cross the Zebrù a second and third time as you continue the hike through alpine forests. At 6,256 feet (1,989 meters) you pass two more refuges and eventually make your way to Baita del Pastone, a lookout point at the foot of Mount Zebrù. Shortly thereafter the trail leaves the woods and runs alongside the River Rio Marè, taking you to the Rifugio V Alpini (9,442 feet/2,878 meters) on Mount Zebrù. You return along the same route.

VAL RABBI ROUTE (trails 41 and 48)

Distance: 6.8 miles (11 kilometers)
Hiking time: 5 hours
High point: 6,975 feet (2,121 meters)
Map: Parco Nazionale dello Stelvio, Touring Club Italiano

The Rabbi Route, which begins in the village of Bagni di Rabbi, is best traveled between June and mid-October when weather conditions are good. In the village there is a park information center along with parking, picnic and camping facilities. From the parking area, take path 48 in a northwestern direction through pine forests. Eventually you will exit the woods, coming out into open meadows with a splendid view of the surrounding mountains. To the left is a cascade which, if you have the time, is worth visiting. Also on the slope ahead is Malga Stablaz Alta (6,758 feet/2,060 meters), a tiny settlement of mountain folk. From here the trail heads north, entering and exiting the nearby woods a couple of times before you encounter the Malghetto di Forborida (6,975 feet/2,121

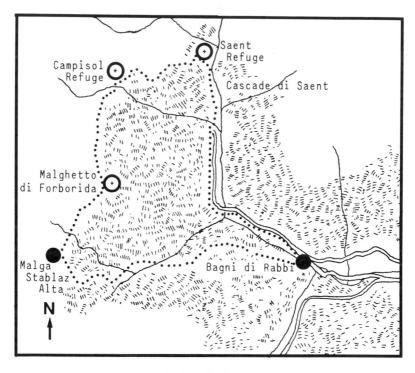

Val Rabbi Route

meters) refuge. The route, designated by black and red painted indicators, becomes extremely panoramic, with waterfalls, impressive rock formations and the woods to your right. At the Campisol Refuge you again enter the forest, soon encountering the Saent Refuge. Here you pick up 41, heading south. Soon you will pass the Cascade di Saent to the left. From here it is a winding, wooded hike past various points of interest, a camping area, and back to the starting point of your journey.

VAL DI LASA HIKE (trail 128)

Distance: 11 miles (17 kilometers)
Hiking time: 6 hours
High point: 6,870 feet (2,094 meters)
Map: Parco Nazionale dello Stelvio, Touring Club Italiano

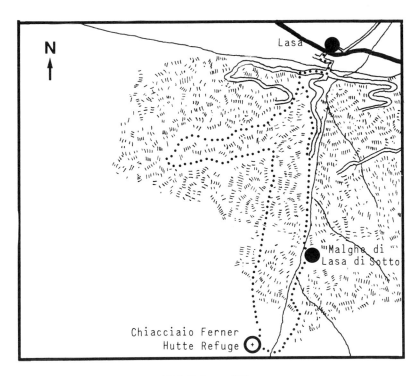

Val di Lasa Hike

The 11 mile (17 kilometer) Val di Lasa hike, along alpine trail
128, is best traveled in July, August and September. Ninety-
five percent of the route is through woods. It begins at the
main road in the town of Lasa and heads south, making a
quick left turn then again going south into the woods. After
making a large "U", the trail forks; you take the left path
running parallel to the Lasa-Laaser Bach River. Halfway into
the hike, at 5,987 feet (1,825 meters), you will pass the mountain settlement of Malghe di Lasa di Sotto. Shortly thereafter,
you exit the woods and reach the Chiacciaio Ferner Hutte Refuge (6,870 feet/2,094 meters). This is an excellent panoramic
point. Here route 128 turns north, soon becoming surrounded
by forest. After slightly more than one hour, you again come to
the fork which you passed earlier. Turn left here and follow the
path back to Lasa.

SEBELWALD HIKE (trail 123)

Distance: 2.5 miles (4 kilometers)
Walking time: 3.15 hours
High point: 6,801 feet (2,073 meters)
Map: Parco Nazionale dello Stelvio, Touring Club Italiano

The Sebelwald hike is good for those who have little time or just want to stretch their legs a bit. The route is not long, but it is uphill—from 5,587 feet (1703 meters) to 6,801 feet (2073 meters)—during the going phase. Fortunately the return is all downhill. The route (alpine trail 123) begins in the village of Masi di Sopra, near the elementary school. From here it heads south-west through picturesque forests, eventually reaching

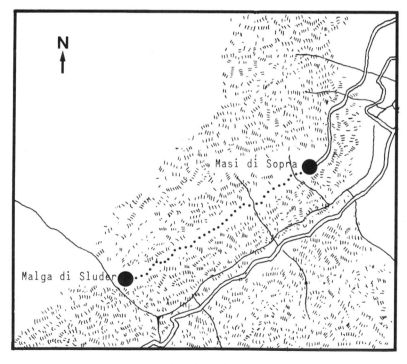

Sebelwald Hike

the mountain settlement of Malga di Sluder. From here, you return via the same route.

LAKE PIÀN PALÙ ROUTE (trails 168 and 32)

Distance: 5.6 miles (9 kilometers)
Walking time: 3 hours
High point: 6,909 feet (2,106 meters)
Map: Parco Nazionale dello Stelvio, Touring Club Italiano

Piàn Palù is a mountain lake surrounded by beautiful forests. This route begins in Fontanino di Celentino, heading south-west towards Lake Piàn Palù. After a short winding trail, you will see the lake on your right. Follow around the south shore of the lake and through the woods at the far side, where you

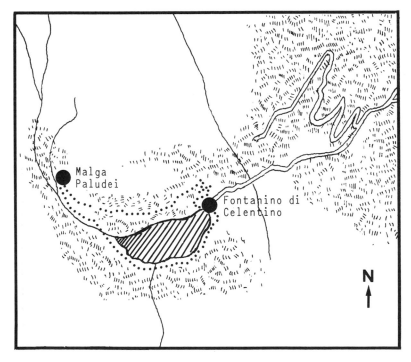

Lake Piàn Palù Route

take alpine route 32. The trail leads to the lookout point at Malga Paludei, a tiny mountain center, before making a "U" and returning along the north shore of Lake Piàn Palù, eventually ending in Fontanino di Celentino.

VALLE ALPISELLA TRAIL (trails 180 and 179)

Distance: 14.9 miles (24 kilometers)
Walking time: 6 hours
High point: 7,529 feet (2,295 meters)
Map: Parco Nazionale dello Stelvio, Touring Club Italiano

The Valle Alpisella trail begins in the town of Livigno. Take the road heading towards Lake di Livigno, next to the church of S. Maria. After passing over the canal, follow the lake's

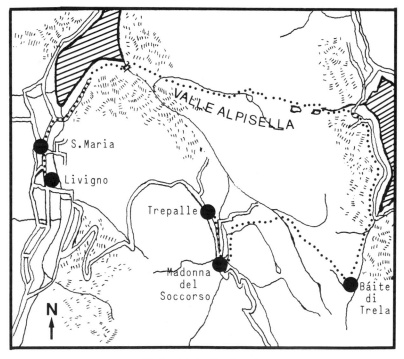

Valle Alpisella Trail

southern shore around and over the Torto canal by means of the Capre Bridge. Trail 180 then takes you into the woods. After 40 minutes you exit the forest and walk through picturesque mountain meadows past the tiny Lake dell'Alpisella, through the Valle Alpisella Pass, and eventually reach Lake S. Giàcomo di Fraele. Here, take the alpine trail 179 south to the tiny center of Baite di Trela. The route turns here, heading north-west along the Val Pila. After passing the high point of the route at the Val Trela Pass, you head downhill until the trail winds into the city of Trepalle. From here local transportation runs to Livigno, where you may have left your automobile.

Abruzzo National Park

Located in central Italy's Apennine mountain range west of Roccaraso in the regions of Abruzzo, Lazio and Molise, the Abruzzo National Park is an outdoor paradise many travelers overlook. Those who discover the park, though, find that no matter what the season there is always something for the outdoor-minded adventurer.

The park consists of 148,200 protected acres of land ranging from 2,625 to 7,365 feet (800 to 2,245 meters) in altitude. The park belongs to 18 municipalities and includes 5 villages with a total of 5,000 inhabitants.

It is zoned into 4 categories:

Zone A—This is the most important from the naturalist's point of view. Here are concentrated the rare or endangered species. It is forbidden to disturb anything in this area; observation of the environment is possible only from footpaths, and in some areas only with the supervision of a park guide.

Zone B—This is the general reserve and includes most of the park (60%). Some villagers are allowed to cut designated trees here for firewood or home building. This zone is considered the meeting point between man and nature.

Zone C—The agricultural zone, these areas are often private, including the lower lands—generally below 3,937 feet (1,200

Emblem of the Abruzzo National Park.

meters) elevation. Here cultivation and animal breeding take place.

Zone D—These are the villages. Park management is trying to implement a plan for each village to have a visitor's center where one can obtain maps and general information about the park. Currently such offices have been established in the larger centers and operate from 9 a.m. to 12 noon and 4 p.m. to 8 p.m.

Sixty percent of the park is forest, 30 percent high meadows and rivers. The majority of the forests are beech, though in the lower elevations many species of mixed oak exist. One can also see Australian pine, Swiss mountain pine, and birch.

In the park are more than 1,200 different species of flowers, some very rare.

Animal life includes 40 different mammal species, 300 birds and 30 reptiles and amphibians. Animals you may see are

In the Abruzzo National Park.

brown bear, wolf, chamois, golden eagle, wild cat, otter, marten, badger, hare, polecat, black squirrel, alpine chough, goshawk, buzzard, eagle owl, and several species of woodpecker including the rare white-backed woodpecker.

During the last 12 years, red deer were reintroduced in hopes of establishing a balanced population. Similarly, lynx, which were killed off several years ago, are being reintroduced.

To protect the quantity and quality of its wildlife, the Abruzzo National Park maintains regulations regarding fishing, hunting, campfires and the discarding of garbage. You can obtain a copy of these regulations by writing L'Ente Autonomo Parco Nationale d'Abruzzo, Vicolo del Curato, 6, 00186 Rome; or the Regione Abruzzo-Assessorato al Turismo, Viale G. Bovio, 65100 Pescara.

There are 154 marked hiking trails within the park. Some routes are short, leisurely walks while others extend through miles of undisturbed nature, over rolling hills and mountain peaks more than 6,561 feet (2,000 meters) high. There are several maps available which include hiking itineraries, plus a series of single-day hikes published by the park administration. They also put out a comprehensive 150-route tourist map of the park. The Touring Club Italiano has a map with several routes, as well as information on the plants, animals and geography of the Abruzzo Park.

PASSAGGIO DELL'ORSO TRAIL (trails 01 and 04)

Distance 11.5 miles (18.5 kilometers)
Hiking time: 5–6 hours
High point: 5,485 feet (1,672 meters)
Map: Parco Nazionale d'Abruzzo, Touring Club Italiano

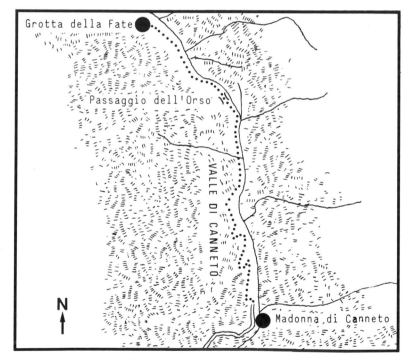

Passaggio dell'Orso Trail

From the city of Settefrati, you can drive or use the public transportation system to get to the church of Madonna di Canneto at 3,350 feet (1,021 meters). Once here, your hiking venture begins along the well-maintained route (designated by 01 indications painted on rocks and trees) heading north into the Valley of Canneto. The trail slowly inclines to your left as you travel parallel to the River Melfa on your right and eventually reaches the Fonte Acquanero (fountain of black water) at 4,350 feet (1,326 meters). The trail continues in a northerly direction through the Valley Tre Confini, between the Mari and Petroso mountains. At one point, the trail divides. Follow the trail to the right (designated 04). This will take you through wooded terrain, moving steadily upward until you reach 1,672 meters at the Passaggio dell'Orso (Bear's Pass). After this panoramic point, the trail begins a drop through the Val Fondillo before it ends at the Grotta della Fate (Cave of the Fairy). This cave is well worth seeing before beginning your return trip along the same route by which you arrived.

CAMPITELLI-META ROUTE (trails L1 and M1)

Distance: 7 miles (11.3 kilometers)
Hiking time: 5 hours
Highest point: 6,500 feet (1,981 meters)
Map: Parco Nazionale d'Abruzzo, Touring Club Italiano

From the town of Alfedena, follow the paved road to the Campitelli Refuge. If you are driving, you can leave your car here. Facing north, you'll notice that camping is allowed on the hill to your left. Directly ahead trail L1 begins (route indicators are located on rocks and trees). Quickly the trail enters the woods and follows a steady incline. For the first hour you will travel along a branch of the Rio Torto river, to your right. Eventually you leave the forest, coming to an open meadow and a splendid view of the Meta peak. Even in the height of summer remnants of snow can be found here. To the right of the trail, just after leaving the woods, are the rock remains of an ancient war refuge. Continue along the route, through the valley towards the Meta. After roughly 2 hours you will come

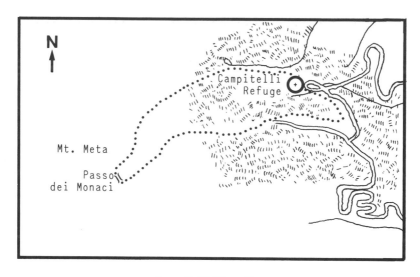

Campitelli-Meta Route

to the Passo dei Monaci bridge at 6,500 feet (1,981 meters). Here there is an excellent panoramic view and you are likely to see wildlife. At this point, you begin your descent along route M1 through the Pagana Valley. Shortly you will reenter the forest and, at about 4 hours into your journey, encounter the spring of Forme at 4,642 feet (1,415 meters). The trail eventually runs through the open Vallefiorita, turning to the left and inclining slightly upward until the Campitelli Refuge comes into view.

LAGO VIVO TRAIL (trails K3, K4, K5, K6)

Distance: 9.5 miles (15 kilometers)
Hiking time: 6 hours
High point: 5,220 feet (1,591 meters)
Map: Parco Nazionale d'Abruzzo, Touring Club Italiano

From the town of Alfedena, take route SS Marsicana N83 to Colle della Croce at 3,832 feet (1,168 meters). If you are driving, you can leave your car in the parking area. From here the

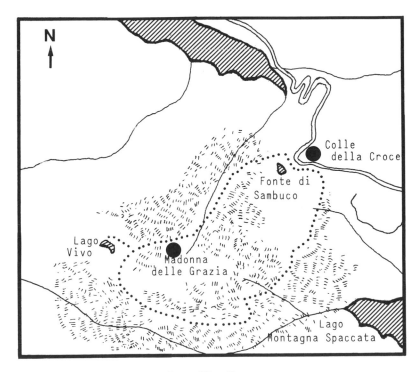

Lago Vivo Route

route (designated K3) heads south-west across open meadows towards Lago Montagna Spaccata (Split Mountain Lake). After 50 minutes, you get a view of the lake to your left prior to entering the forest. The route inclines upward here, running parallel to the Rio Torto stream. Another 45 minutes of walking and the trail turns west into the wooded Porcile Valley, passing by bridge over the Rio and heading uphill through the valley. Continue to follow the K3 indicators through the picturesque woods for another 90 minutes. At this point the trail begins to turn to the right in a northern course and, after 2 large bends, turns left onto trail K4. Continuing to the northwest you will leave the forest, passing through a valley and, at the opposite side of the opening, come upon a trail to the left leading to Lake Vivo (5,220 feet-1,591 meters). The lake is often dry during the summer but beautiful at other times of the year and well worth the sidetrip. After visiting the lake, return to the main trail and follow it left (north-east) into the woods. At this point the route becomes K5—be sure those are the markers you follow. You'll begin to descend now through the Valley of Infermo, passing the Madonna delle Grazia chapel to the right and eventually leave the woods at the Sorgente delle Donne (Spring of Women). Turning right onto Route K6 you'll travel through lightly wooded zones and open meadows, pass the Fountain of Sambuco on your right, and finally return to Colle della Croce where the hike began.

VALLELONGA HIKE (trail R1)

Distance: 12 miles (19 kilometers)
Hiking time: 3–4 hours
High point: 3,947 feet (1,203 meters)
Map: Parco Nazionale d'Abruzzo, Touring Club Italiano

From the town of Villavallelonga, where there is a visitor's information center, animal preserve and park museum, continue south-west along the valley road to the Madonna della Lanna chapel, at an altitude of 3,563 feet (1,086 meters). If driving, you can park your auto here. There is also an area for camping to the left of the trail. From the church, the paved road continues for another mile (1.6 kilometers). Then, following the R1 markers, you proceed along the forest trail, parallel to the Torrente Rosa stream. Soon you exit the woods into the Prati d'Angro, an area once known for its lynx population. If you are fortunate you may encounter deer here. The trail crosses the meadow, following the stream and forest borders until you reach the Aceretta Refuge at 3,947 feet (1,203 meters). From here you get an excellent view of the Balzo di Ciotto forest to the south. The return trip, which takes about 90 minutes is along the same route.

FONDILLO CAVE HIKE (trail F10)

Distance: 2 miles (3 kilometers)
Hiking time: 1 hour

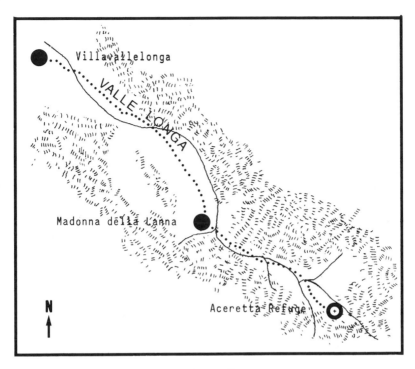

Vallelonga Route

High point: 3,737 feet (1,200 meters)
Map: Parco Nazionale d'Abruzzo, Touring Club Italiano

From highway SS Marsicana N83, east of Opi, trail F10 leads into the Fondillo Valley. Immediately after the River Sangro bridge, there is an old saw mill where you can park your car. Passing through the nearby picnic and camping areas, continue for about 20 minutes until you reach the Fondillo Cave. The thick forest here is known for its population of brown bears. If you are interested in exploring other caves, you can pick up route F2 at this point and extend the hike south through the Fondillo Valley to the Grotta della Fate (4 miles or 6.4 kilometers roundtrip). If not, or when you return from the

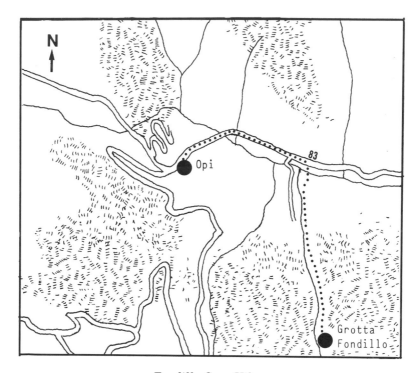

Fondillo Cave Hike

extended excursion, continue along the F10 trail, encountering the Tornareccia natural spring, and eventually returning to your point of origin.

During the summer it is possible to travel the entire Fondillo Valley on horseback. Arrangements can be made at the information office in Opi.

BISEGNA HIKE (trail W1)

Distance: 8.7 miles (14 kilometers)
Hiking Time: 3.30 hours
High point: 5,741 feet (1,750 meters)
Map: Parco Nazionale d'Abruzzo, Touring Club Italiano

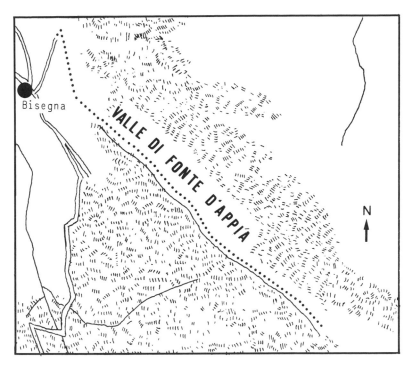

Bisegna Hike

From the village of Bisegna, where an information center and animal preserve have been established, take the Spina Cerreto mountain road upwards for 1.5 miles (2.5 kilometers) until you reach the Valley of the Appia Fountain at 4,465 feet (1,361 meters). If you are traveling by auto, leave the vehicle here. Continue on foot along trail W1 in a south-eastern direction, which soon leads you into the forest. After crossing two small streams—which may be dry during the summer—you come into an open meadow. From here the trail continues upwards to a lookout point at 5,741 feet (1,750 meters). For those who would like to continue still further, it is possible to climb Monte Grande, on the left, to a height of 7,050 feet (2,149 meters) for a breathtaking view. To return, retrace your route.

PIAZZALE DELLA CAMOSCIARA TRAIL (trails G1, G5, G6)

Distance: 4.7 miles (7.5 kilometers)
Hiking time: 2.30 hours
High point: 4,715 feet (1,437 meters)
Map: Parco Nazionale d'Abruzzo, Touring Club Italiano

This trail begins in the village of Villetta. From here, take state Highway Marsicana N83 west towards Opi for 1.9 miles (3 kilometers). Here, a road leads off to the left, heading south. After crossing the River Sangro bridge there are camping and parking areas. If you have driven from Villetta, your automobile can be left here. Or you can drive further along the dirt

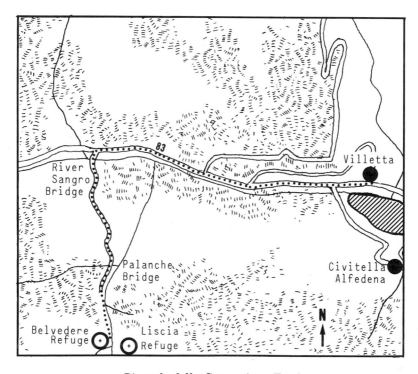

Piazzale della Camosciara Trail

road and park your car after the bridge of Palanche (this road, however, is sometimes closed). From the first parking area follow the indicators for trail G1 through an open meadow. To your left, the Scerto stream runs parallel to the route. Soon you will pass over the bridge of Palanche—the second parking area is on your right—and enter the birch and pine forest. You are now at the Piazzale delle Camosciara. At this point, several routes merge, including G1, G5 and G6. Take route G5 to the left which will lead you to the Tre Cannelle waterfalls. After visiting the falls, return to the Piazzale and turn left onto route G6. Along the way are various minor cascades, including the Cascade of the Ninfe. The route constantly inclines upward, heading south towards Mount Capraro. At the end of the trail you will come to the Belvede and Liscia Refuges at an altitude of 4,715 feet (1,437 meters). The view here is breathtaking. This is a perfect location for viewing wildlife such as Abruzzo chamois and royal eagle. The return trip is via the same route.

RIFUGIO DEL DIAVOLO (trail T1)

Distance: 7.5 miles (12 kilometers)
Hiking time: 3 hours
High point: 4,741 feet (1,445 meters)
Map: Parco Nazionale d'Abruzzo, Touring Club Italiano

The Rifugio del Diavolo hike begins, naturally enough, at the Refuge of the Devil, 6 miles (10 kilometers) north of Pescasseroli off state Highway Marsicana N83. The refuge is situated on the left, just after the Passo del Diavolo bridge. You will also find parking and picnic areas there. Route T1 heads south through the Penna meadow, turning right before the Spineto woods. The altitude here is 4,619 feet (1,408 meters). Continuing on a south-western course the trail, bordered by woods, eventually turns north-west, entering a wooded area where a few years ago speculators constructed villas. Fortunately. the construction was stopped and today only a few remnants can be seen among the trees. At an altitude of 5,013 feet (1,528 meters) you'll leave the forest, entering an open area known as

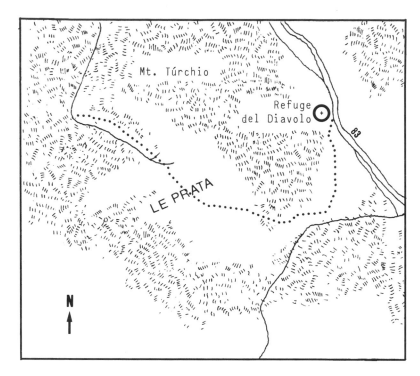

Rifugio de Diavolo

the Prata at the foot of Mount Turchio, which can be seen ahead and to the right. Again you enter the forest, passing over two streams (following them to the right will bring you to the tiny springs from which they originate) and eventually reach the Cava di Bauxite, an old mining site located at 4,741 feet (1,445 meters). Along the route, several trails branch off from, or cross, T1. So be sure to follow the markers carefully. Return via the same route.

National Park of Circeo Hikes

The National Park of Circeo was formed in 1934 and although one of the smallest and most populated of the Italian National

Welcome to the National Park of Circeo.

Parks, it is certainly the one that contains the greatest number of riches. It is famous not only because of its extremely interesting ecological situation, but because of the many anthropological and archaeological remains of civilizations that have flourished in this area since prehistoric times.

Located near the sea, in west-central Italy, the National Park of Circeo contains 20,748 acres. Among its features are a calcareous headland which overlooks the Tyrrhenian Sea, the last remaining section of an ancient lowland forest, 4 coastal lakes and sand dunes along an 18.6-mile (30-kilometer) stretch of coast. Most recently, Zannone Island was added to the park domain.

The park contains a vast array of flora, including Mediterranean evergreen shrubs and, in the more humid places, deciduous forests of oak. There are also hornbeam, pine, quaking aspen, alder and elm trees. A few examples of ilex and cork exist as well. The area is rich in flowers and various species of fungi, which abound as a result of the wet climate in certain parts of the park.

Mammals of the Circeo Park include wild boar, fallow-deer, fox, polecat, porcupines, hedgehogs, hares, wild rabbits, badgers, otters, weasels, beech-martens and squirrels.

There are also many reptiles found here. Frequently one can see vipers, water snakes, green lizards and both earth and swamp tortoises.

The park is primarily known for the great variety and number of birds, both permanent and migratory. Some of the more noted species include the green woodpecker, the great spotted and the lesser spotted woodpeckers, the nuthatch, the tree creeper and the wood pigeon. Along the sea cliffs you can see the blue rock thrush and alpine swift. There are also many herring gulls and, at times, the rare wall creeper.

Waterbirds in the area, particularly around Lakes Fogliano and Monaci, include the gray heron, the night heron, the stilt and the gull-billed tern. In the spring, autumn and winter, cormorants, widgeons, teals, shovelers, pintails, mallards, garganeys, pochards and many waders are present. On rare occasions one may even get a glimpse of the peregrine falcon.

Getting to the National Park of Circeo

The park is within easy reach of both Rome and Naples.

From Rome take Highway 148 for Latina. From here Sabaudia is a short distance south. From Naples take Highway SS 7 through Gaeta and Terracina, exiting onto Highway 213 to Sabaudia.

Where to Get Information

Obtaining information on the National Park of Circeo is simply a matter of writing the State Agency of Forests, Administration Office, Bureau of Sabaudia, 04016 Italy. Or, prior to venturing out, you can stop at the information center located

Great egret in the National Park of Circeo.

at the entrance to the park in Sabaudia. There is an excellent museum here which will give you a good feel for the park's history. Nearby there are picnic and camping areas.

The Trails

Unlike the hiking trails of some parks in Italy, those of the National Park of Circeo are near sea level. Walking is, therefore, easy. Most of the trails are very well kept and simple to follow. Along some of the routes signs have been posted to provide information on local animals and plants. Unfortunately, these are only in Italian. A few routes are appropriate not only for hiking, but bicycle riding as well. These are indicated at the beginning of the trail. The park management—not the Italian Alpine Club, as is the case in some parks—has assigned check point numbers along each itinerary. Historical sites of interest—old Roman ruins, early settlements, etc.—have been included in many itineraries by park officials. Some of these have even been reconstructed to give hikers a feel for the past. Hiking in Circeo can be enjoyed year-round.

CIRCEO FOREST ROUTE

Distance: 8.7 miles (14 kilometers)
Hiking time: 3 hours
High point: 55.7 feet (17 meters)
Map: Parco Nazionale del Circeo, Touring Club Italiano

The Forest Route begins from the nature center at the north-western corner of the park. There is a parking area here, as well as a picnic zone, park information office and animal study area with local wildlife. Heading out in a south-western direction, you will soon come to check point 5. Continue straight ahead to check point 7. Here, turn left through the woods to check point 10. Take another left here, which will lead you to check point 9. Making a right turn, continue along the forest route until you come to a fork in the trail. Take the left branch.

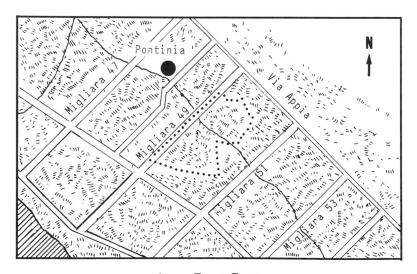

Circeo Forest Route

This makes a "U" around the local nature zone and brings you back to the parking area where you began your excursion.

LAKE SABAUDIA TRAIL

Distance: 3.8 miles (6.2 kilometers)
Hiking time: 2 hours
High point: sea level
Map: Parco Nazionale del Circeo, Touring Club Italiano

This is an interesting route for its historical sights. Beginning at the park information and picnic center in Sabaudia—where you can purchase maps and English-language brochures or visit the park museum—take the trail to check point 20. Passing by a reconstructed early settlement on your right, continue to check point 21. Here there is a crossing of trails. Go straight through the woods. Some tree cutting is being carried out in this area. Eventually the trail branches. Taking the trail ahead will lead you to the shore of Lake Sabaudia. After

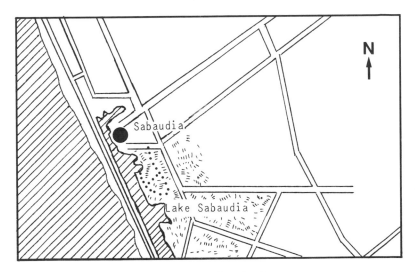

Lake Sabaudia Trail

visiting the lake, return to this point and take the left trail. Depending on the season, this section of the route offers a variety of colorful flora. Soon you will come to check point 23. Continue ahead until you encounter check point 21. From here turn left and return to the park information center.

MONTE CIRCELLO TRAIL

Distance: 2 miles (3.2 kilometers)
Hiking time: 4.20 hours
High point: 1,775 feet (541 meters)
Map: Parco Nazionale del Circeo, Touring Club Italiano

This route takes you up Monte Circello, to one of the finest panoramic points in the park. The trail begins from the San Paolo church along the "Lungomare" (coastal road) and next

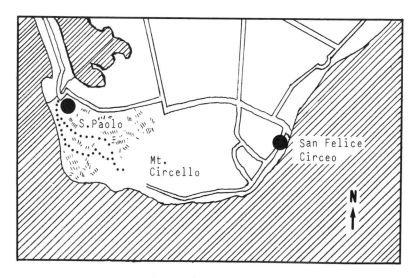

Monte Circello Trail

to the Romano Canal. In the vicinity are: the Torre Paola, a sixteenth-century tower as well as the Grotta Spaccata and the Grotta di Paola, two seaside caves that are worth exploring. Taking the trail through the woods, you begin an uphill walk. At the fork, take the left route. Continue ahead until the trail branches again. Turn right. Another trail soon intersects the one you are on. Keep on a straight course. Just after you exit the woods the trail is again intersected by another route. Take the left trail uphill to the peak of Monte Circello (1,775 feet/ 541 meters). In the process, you will pass the remains of the Temple of Circeo, a sacred place during Roman times. Not far away you can also see the Moresca Tower, built in 1569. After taking in the view, return by the same route which led you to the mountain peak, along the border of the woods and the mountain slope. There are some excellent panoramas here. Eventually the trail branches to the right. Taking this trail will lead you downhill through the woods, where you should take the first left, leading you back to the church of San Paolo.

ZANNONE ISLAND ROUTE

Distance 2 miles (3.2 kilometers)
Hiking time: 2 hours
High point: 636 feet (194 meters)
Map: Parco Nazionale del Circeo, Touring Club Italiano

The Island of Zannone, the most recent addition to the National Park of Circeo, can be reached only by local fishing boats from the island of Ponza. The trip takes about 1 hour. Being of volcanic origin, the island has many interesting natural features. From the port, on the south-western side of the island, a trail heads uphill to the park shelter and the St. Benedict convent. The trail turns right here, running around the slopes of Mount Pellegrino and eventually reaching the 636-foot (194-meter) peak of the mountain. You can then walk down to the park shelter and back to the port.

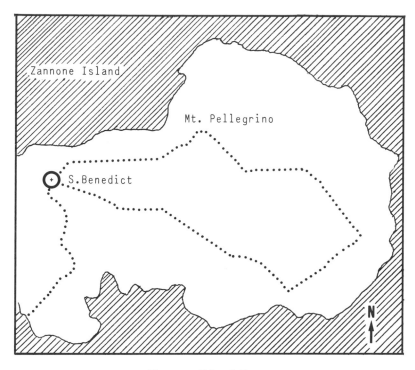

Zannone Island Route

National Park of Calabria Hikes

The National Park of Calabria was founded in 1968, but until recently it did not have management or direction. It was, in effect, a park on paper only. Today, it is administered by the State Agency of Forests. Bureau of Cosenza, Viale della Repubblica 25, Cosenza 87100, Italy.

The park is located in southern Italy's Calabria region, along the Sila Mountain range. It comprises three separate areas: the Sila Grande (17,290 acres); the Sila Piccola (14,820 acres); and the Aspromonte (9,980 acres). The park is composed of granitic rocks covered by coniferous and broadleaved forests. These vary, however, from location to location. Mountain streams, thick forests and picturesque solitude are all

Emblem of the Calabria National Park.

trademarks of the zone.

Hundreds of wild flowers grow within the borders of this 3-section park. Among the trees are pine, beech, European turkey oak, and birch.

The animal life includes wolves, roe-deer, wild cats, boar, black woodpecker, Bonelli eagle and a variety of small mammals.

Getting to the Park

From the north, you can reach the Sila Grande by taking the A3 Autostrada to the Cosenza exit. From here take Highway SS 107 to Camigliatello. Then take SS 177 to Cupone. From

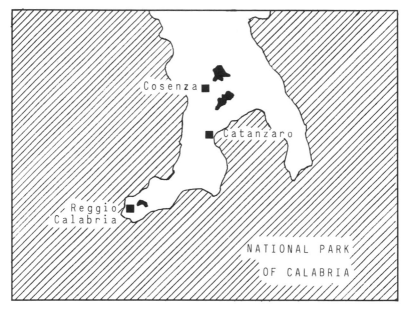

The three zones of the National Park of Calabria.

the east take Highway SS 106 to Mirto Crosia, then SS 177 to Longobucco.

The Sila Piccola can be reached from the north via A3 to Cosenza, SS 107 to Silvana Masio and Lorica, then SS 108 and 179 to Gariglione. From the east take SS 106 to Crotone, SS 107 at Cotronei to Lago Ampollino.

The third area of the park, Aspromonte, can be reached by taking the A3 exit at S. Eufemia d'Aspromonte and SS 183 to Gambarie. Those coming from the east can take SS 106 to Reggio Calabria and SS 183/184 to Gamnarie.

You can also reach these areas by local train from Cosenza and Reggio Calabria.

Where to Get Information

In addition to the park headquarters, listed above, you can

obtain information regarding the park from the: Administration Office, Parco Nazionale di Calabria, Via Cortese, 88100 Catanzaro, Italy; or Administration Office, Parco Nazionale di Calabria, Via Prolungamento Torrione, 89100 Reggio Calabria, Italy.

Hiking and Routes

Because Calabria is the youngest of the country's national parks it is not as developed as the others. While there are some hiking trails, they are not as well-defined or extensive as, say, those within the Abruzzo or Gran Paradiso parks. Trails are being expanded though, and you should contact the central office of the park or the local tourist board for an up-to-date map of the routes available.

This is an excellent area in which to test your outdoor skills. Equipped with a good map—available from local Italian Alpine Clubs and in some of the bookstores in Reggio Calabria—along with a compass and general camping gear, you can establish your own routes and hiking adventures. This brings you face-to-face with natural wonders that planned routes often overlook. Your chances of encountering local wildlife are also greater along trails you blaze yourself.

This type of hiking, however, calls for more planning. If you are not familiar with the workings of a compass and mapping directions, do not attempt setting out on your own. Those who do have the required training should plan their itinerary in advance, based on natural landmarks such as rock formations and rivers, then keep to that route.

PART IV

ITALY'S ISLANDS

Much of Italy's 116,303 square miles (301,225 kilometers) is disbursed among more than 40 islands. Some of the country's islands, such as Sicily and Sardinia, are vast while others like Gorgona and San Domino are little more than hills in the open sea.

Despite the varied sizes, Italy's islands hold one thing in common: they offer adventure. From diving and delving into active volcanos, to hiking and spelunking, you'll find it well worth your while to explore them.

Footloose on Capri

Some call it the playground of the jet set. Others, the jewel of Naples Bay or the island of wonders. Whatever the title, most visitors look upon Capri as a hodge-podge of tourists, sunbathers and aristocrats. During the months of June, July and August, this is a fairly accurate description. At other times, though, the island becomes a hiker's paradise, offering solitude, tranquility and natural beauty.

Capri has been inhabited from the early Paleolithic age (25,000 B.C.). In classical times the island was a Greek colony and later became a summer resort for Roman rulers. One of the memorable events in the island's history occured in 29

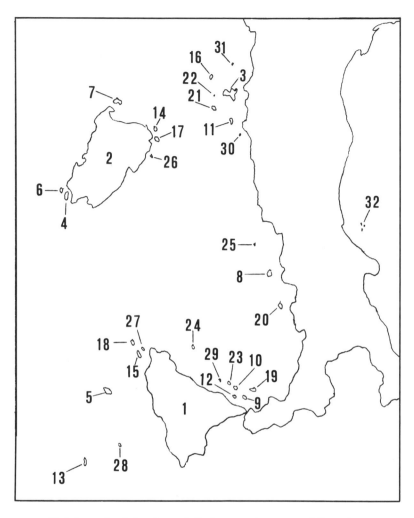

Italy's major islands and their areas in square kilometers.

1. Sicily 25,462
2. Sardinia 23,813
3. Elba 223
4. Sant'Antioco 109
5. Pantelleria 83
6. San Pietro 51
7. Asinari 51

8. Ischia 46
9. Lipari 37
10. Salina 26
11. Giglio 21
12. Vulcano 21
13. Lampedusa 20
14. La Maddalena 20

15. *Favignana 20*	24. *Ustica 8*
16. *Capraia 19*	25. *Ponza 7*
17. *Caprera 16*	26. *Tavolara 6*
18. *Maréttino 12*	27. *Lèvanzo 6*
19. *Stromboli 12*	28. *Linosa 5*
20. *Capri 10*	29. *Alicudi 5*
21. *Montecristo 10*	30. *Giannutri 2*
22. *Pianosa 10*	31. *Gorgona 2*
23. *Filicudi 9*	32. *San Domino 2*

B.C. when Caesar Augustus, after a visit to Capri, was so struck with its natural beauty that he acquired it from the city of Naples in exchange for its larger and wealthier sister island, Ischia. Tiberius, successor to Augustus, constructed 12 villas here which were to represent the 12 divinities of Olympus; and from the most important of these, Villa Jovis, he ruled the whole Roman Empire for 10 years. After Tiberius, rulers and nobles continued to frequent the island and its imperial villas until the 6th century. At that point the island reverted back to the Duchy of Naples. In the years that followed, Capri passed into the hands of Saracens, Lombards, Normans, Angevins, Aragonese, Spaniards, French and British. In 1800, the final invasion began: by artists, writers, poets, naturalists, and backpackers.

Getting to Capri

From the city of Naples there are ferries to Capri which leave from the Molo Beverello, in front of the Castle Maschio Angioino in Piazza Municipio, beginning at 7 a.m. On clear days the ferries offer a delightful ride. Several of the boats have coffee bars as well as indoor and outdoor seating accommodations. There are also hydrofoil boats, which cut your 17-mile (27.6-kilometer) sea trip from an hour and a half to 45 minutes. These depart from the same location about every 2 hours. The cost of the hydrofoil is slightly higher.

Hydrofoils (the SNAV Lines) run daily from the Naples

Mergellina, also on Via Caracciolo. Daily boats leave Amalfi and Sorrento as well every 3 hours for Capri.

All arriving boats pull into the Marina Grande, on Capri's north side. During the low tourist season there are normally several hotels with available accommodations. The island is divided into two sections—Capri and Anacapri. If you are planning to see the island on foot, try to stay in the "town" of Capri, since most walks begin here.

CAPRI'S SOUTH-EASTERN ROUTE

Distance: 4.5 miles (7.24 kilometers)
Hiking time: 5–6 hours
Highest point: 1,095 feet (334 meters)

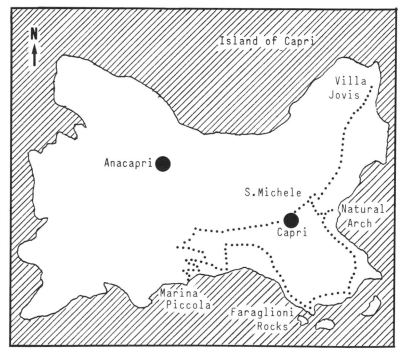

Capri's South-Eastern Route

This route takes you along paved or brick trails designed for walking and on some of the island's black-topped roads. Because it is unlawful to drive a car on Capri unless you are a resident, roads are used very little and wind through some very nice countryside.

Beginning in Piazza Umberto I, the main square in the town of Capri, follow Via Le Botteghe uphill until you come to a crossroad. Follow Via Tiberio uphill. The San Michele church will be on your left as the road continues to climb through picturesque vineyards, finally coming to the Villa Jovis at the top of Mount Tiberio (1,095 feet/334 meters). Because of rock formations and sudden drops, you will find there is much back-tracking required on the island's trails.

From the Villa Jovis, return down Via Tiberio to Piazza La Croce. Take the road to the left, which is Via Matromania, putting you on a south-eastern course. This route leads to the unique phenomenon of geologic erosion known as the Natural Arch. A few feet away from the arch is an antique stairway leading down to the Cave of Matromania. This was hollowed out of the east side of the island's coast by centuries of water movement. The cave forms a semicircular apse with several smaller chambers.

From here continue down the steps for about 65 feet (20 meters). On your right is a well-maintained path which will take you along a winding coastal route. After 15 or 20 minutes of hiking along these so-called Pizzolungo Cliffs, you'll come to Porto Tragara where a platform overlooks the famed Faraglioni Rocks, the Marina Piccola and Monte Solaro.

If you wish, you can take the tiny beaten path at the right of the platform down to the sea and examine the remains of an old Roman port. You will, however, have to re-climb the cliff you originally descended to return to the main route.

Continuing along the path, through the cliffs in a north-western direction, you eventually come to the asphalted Via Tragara. This road winds along some beautiful pine groves and wooded areas before ending in the town of Capri, where it becomes Via Camerelle. After entering the town, continue through the first and second crossroads. Just past the second intersection watch for the Quisisana Hotel. To the right of the

hotel is a narrow cobblestone lane leading to the Gardens of Augustus. Here, during the Roman period, beautiful flowers and other ornamental plants were cultivated. From here a 20-minute walk down the Via Krupp—32 feet (10 meters) to the west—takes you into Marina Piccola with its small beaches and towering cliffs.

The route next goes up Via Marina Piccola, an asphalted road. After about 20 minutes, you will find steps leading off to the right. By following these to the end, you will come out on the Via Roma which, if you turn right, will take you into town.

CAPRI'S WESTERN ROUTE

Distance: 4 miles (6.4 kilometers)
Hiking time: 5–6 hours
Highest point: 1,932 feet (589 meters)

Like the previous trail, Capri's Western Route consists of paved or brick walking trails, with some walking on asphalt roads through picturesque surroundings.

From the town of Capri, walk up the Via Provinciale Anacapri which begins on the west side of town. This beautiful 40-minute walk offers views of the gulf of Naples from the Sorrentine Peninsula to the island of Ischia. At the point where the road passes the Chapel of St. Anthony on the right, you turn left onto Viale A. Munthe. Taking it, you will come to Piazza della Vittoria where you can take a chair-lift to the top of Mount Solaro. At 1,932 feet (589 meters), this is the island's highest vista.

At the top of the mountain there is a well-maintained path for descending. Heading in a northern direction, the path winds through a tiny valley before it comes out at the chapel of Santa Maria Cetrella—dating to the 14th century—after which it descends into Anacapri. From Piazza della Vittoria, continue along the little path which branches off from the far left corner. This is Via Migliara and runs along the slopes of Mount Solaro up to the Belvedere della Migliara, a lookout

Along Capri's South-Eastern Route.

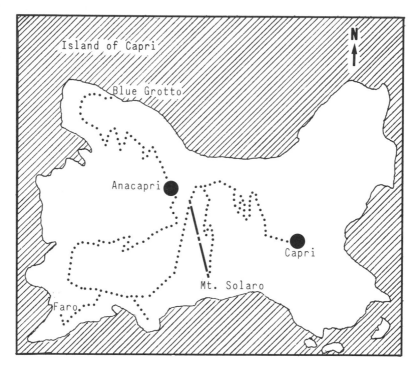

Capri's Western Route

point overlooking the precipices of Point Carene (40 minutes on foot). From this summit you will get a bird's-eye view of the Faraglioni Rocks to the left and the inlet of the Green Grotto.

Next, backtrack slightly, turning left so that you head west on the Via Migliara. The road makes a large curve and swings north to intersect with Strada del Fero di Carena. This paved road leads to the Punto Cerena lighthouse if you turn left and take it to the end. It is a relaxing, downhill walk. After visiting the lighthouse. however, you will need to backtrack.

Continuing up the Strada del Fero di Carena, you will pass the ancient remains of the "Torre della Guarda," a Roman lookout tower where soldiers were posted to guard against at-

The Western Route on Capri offers breathtaking views.

tacks, and the double archway known as "Torre di Materita." The road eventually leads to Anacapri.

From the town's main square, now take Via Pagliaro—a new asphalt road which leads to the sea and the renowned Blue Grotto through orchards and vineyards. Following a visit to the mysterious cavern, you may return by the same route or catch a boat that will take you to the Marina Grande along the island's picturesque northern coast.

Capri's South-Eastern and Western routes can usually be covered in 2 good days. The routes, however, are designed so that you can easily delete portions should you find yourself running late. For example, the South-Eastern route can be separated in to the Villa Jovis-Mount Tiberio trail (2 hours), the Natural Arch-Matromania Cave-Pizzolungo trail (2 hours 15 minutes), and the Certosa-Gardens of Augustus trail (1 hour 30 minutes). Any of these routes may be taken as separate walks or together as proposed above. The perfect situation is to allow 3 days and combine the routes to suit your schedule.

Maps and Information

Walking has become such a popular pastime on Capri that the local tourist board has prepared a special brochure, in English, with 9 hiking itineraries (most of which have been described above) and maps. The walks cover the entire island. The brochure, and other maps, are available from the Azienda Autonoma di Soggiorno e Turismo, in Piazza Cerio (tel. 837–0424), or the Tourist Information Offices at Marina Grande (tel. 837–0634) and Piazza Umberto 1 (tel. 837–0686). To obtain copies of the hiking maps before going to the island, write or visit the ENTE Provinciale per il Turismo, Via Partenope 10A, 80121 Naples, Italy.

Sicily

There is something magical about Sicily. The power and fire-

Capri's I Faraglioni

belching magnificence of Mount Etna creates fear in the bravest of men. The ancient splendors of Syracuse leave historians in awe. Archaeologists take on a childish air as they gaze upon Agrigento's Valley of the Temples. Voyagers become Odysseus-like explorers as they maneuver through the luring waters of the Aeolian Islands. Those who do not fall victim to such spell-casting attractions often find themselves being tantalized into gastronomic feasts where sweet, sparkling wines eventually work their magic. Don't fight the charm of Sicily. Instead, do as millions have done before you—relax, explore, absorb the emotions, the aromas, the tastes, and enjoy it all.

The largest island in the Mediterranean, covering an area of about 10,000 square miles (25,900 kilometers), Sicily must be observed in small doses to be truly enjoyed. Because of its vastness, travelers often find it advantageous to limit their adventures to selected attractions and/or areas.

The Italian government has established 5 protected areas on Sicily, the largest of which is the National Park of Etna. This

60,000 acre park surrounds the Mount Etna volcano.

In addition to the thrill of volcano exploring (see Part IX, "Hot Foot Adventures") this zone is noted for its abundance of wildlife including rabbits, foxes and a variety of birds. On the southern slopes, near Monte Vetore, there are the Nuova Gussonea Botanic Gardens; to the north and west are caves such as the Grotta delle Palombe, Grotta del Gelo, Grotta della Vanelle, and Grotta della Neve.

You can enjoy snow skiing, speleology, and climbing here—in addition to hiking, camping, and volcano exploring. Something that has become popular among local adventurers is dry, downhill skiing on the volcanic sand found in various sections of Etna. The Italian Alpine Club in Catania (address in Appendix D) can provide the exact locations for such activities as well as guides.

Another popular activity in the park is hang-gliding. The Centro Volo Libero Etna Delta (Via Diana 124, 95013 Fiumefreddo CT, Italy), provides hang gliders (with or without motor), as well as sport parachutes for those interested. If you have never participated in such sports, they also offer bilingual lessons. Besides the Mount Etna site, the club has offices in Taormina, Palermo, Caltagirone and Siracusa.

For organized hiking, as part of a group or independently, Hiking International (see Appendix A for a complete listing of outfitters) is highly recommended. They offer 11-day itineraries complete with maps, tips, and prearrangements, including accommodations and meals.

Practical Information

Maps and information on Sicily can be obtained by writing the regional tourist board (address in Appendix C) or the following Provincial Tourist offices:

PALERMO—Piazza Castelnuovo 35, 90100 Palermo
TRAPANI—Via Vito Sorba 15, 91100 Trapani
AGRIGENTO—Viale della Vittoria 255, 92100 Agrigento

Volcanic activity on Mt. Etna.

Mt. Etna hovers like a ghost image over Sicily's countryside.

RAGUSA—Via Natalelli 131, 97100 Ragusa
CATANIA—Largo Paisiello 5, 95124 Catania
SYRACUSE—Via S. Sebastiano 43, 96100 Siracusa
CALTANISSETTA—Corso Vittorio Emmanuele 109, 93100 Caltanissetta
ENNA—Piazza Garibaldi, 94100 Enna
MESSINA—Via Calabria is. 301/Bis, 98100 Messina

Sardinia

Separated from mainland Italy by miles of limpid blue Mediterranean water, Sardinia is an island that, in many respects, time has forgotten. Its inhabitants are simple people maintaining many of the traditions of their ancestors.

Among the island's 9,300 square miles (24,087 square kilometers), are rugged mountains, clean white beaches, thick wooded regions, isolated brush-lands, open meadows, unexplored caves and canyons and picturesque lagoons. Sardinia is a paradise of unspoiled nature. Here you can find flamingos, eagles, vultures, deer, boar, mountain sheep, porcupines, seals, sea turtles, whales and one of the world's last herds of wild horses.

Because Sardinia draws thousands of adventure-seeking visitors each year, several outfitters offer excursions to the island. One of the finest is Sardegna da Scoprire. This outfit will provide you with maps, itineraries, gear and advice for "on-your-own" adventures or guided group outings. They offer hiking, horseback trekking, speleology and canoeing. Horseback ventures can also be arranged through Alabirdi (Strada a Mare 24, 09021 Arborea, Oristano, Italy, tel. 0783/48268); A.N.T.E. (Sardegna, Via Pasteur 4, 09100 Cagliari, tel. 070/305816) and Trekking International. In addition, the latter offers week-long hiking adventures in Sardinia, as does Hiking International. For more information on mountain excursions, as well as local hiking and climbing conditions, contact the Club Alpino Italiano in Cagliara (address in Appendix D). For canoe trips, Club Avventour is your best bet. More information on these and other outfitters can be found in Appendix A.

Sardinia contains 5 wildlife reserves—Caprera, Capo Caccia, Sinis, Monte Arcosu and Molentargius. Most adventurers, however, prefer the sites and activities found in the proposed National Park of Gennargentu.

Proposed National Park of Gennargentu

Located in central Sardinia, south of Nuoro, this proposed National Park takes in more than 100,000 acres of practically uninhabited wild land, including coastal regions, mountains, and forests. Here you can explore, camp, climb, and canoe for days without encountering another human being. Because of the varied terrain, many species of animals and plants are found here.

Those seeking a glimpse of the island's wild horses would do best to venture along the 1,640–1,968-foot/500–600-meter-high basalt plateau known as Giara. Seven and a half miles (12.7 kilometers) long and 3 miles (4.8 kilometers) wide, Giara is located a short distance from the town of Barumin on Highway 197. For this venture, the assistance of a specialized guide is suggested to save time and insure you find the roaming herds. Guides can be arranged through the Italian Alpine Club in Cagliari (address in Appendix D) or the city halls in the towns of Gesturi and Tuili.

Maps and information about the National Park of Gennargentu and surrounding areas can be obtained from: Ente Provinciale per il Turismo, Piazza Deffenu 9, 09100 Cagliari; Azienda Autonoma di Soggiorno e Turismo, Piazza Matteotti 1, 09100 Cagliari; and the provincial tourist office at Piazza Italia 19, 08100 Nuoro. Material on the entire island can be obtained from the regional tourist office (address in Appendix C).

In addition to information on Sardinia's wild lands, tourist offices offer a large selection of English-language brochures,

Sardinia's flamingos.

including regional itineraries for motorists, cyclists, and hikers. (See bicycling itineraries in Part V).

There are 3 major forest ranges on the island: the Forest of Seven Brothers (11 acres) in the south; the Montarbu Forest (7 acres) in the central region; and the Goceano Forest (10 acres) to the north. Each is overseen by a ranger station and camping is permitted upon written request. For more information on Sardinia's forest excursions, as well as camp permits, write to the Ufficio Amministrazione Foreste Demaniali. For Seven Brothers Forest the address is: Via Nuoro 72, 09100 Cagliari; for Montarbu Forest, Via Trieste 08100 Nuoro; for Goceano Forest, Via Sanna 25, 07100 Sassari.

Sardinia can be reached by air or sea. The island is serviced by Alitalia, ATI, Alisarda and Aermediterranea airlines, which are linked with major airports on the mainland and fly into Alghero, Olbia and Cagliari. Terrenia and Trans Tirreno Express ship lines service Sardinia from Genova, Livorno, Civitavecchia, Naples, Palermo and Trapani. Vessels run daily to Porto Torres, Olbia, Arbatax and Cagliari.

THE GORROPU CANYON ADVENTURE

Situated on the eastern coast of Sardinia, in the province of Nuoro, is the Rio Flumineddu, a river that through the ages has created the Gorropu, a 10-mile/16-kilometer-long canyon running south to north. This offers one of the finest adventures in all of Italy.

Taking on the Gorropu Canyon requires a number of skills: climbing, rafting, backpacking, speleology and a knowledge of survival techniques. Here one finds isolated solitude, rich flora, a river that evolves from a tiny passage to a series of crystal clear pools, an underground lake and wide caverns. The canyon contains a variety of unique and often breathtaking rock formations.

In addition to general backpacking gear, this adventure calls for light climbing equipment, a small rubber boat (the type used by children will be fine as long as you can fit inside), and a hammock that can be strung between rock formations for sleeping. A good supply of fresh water should also be included.

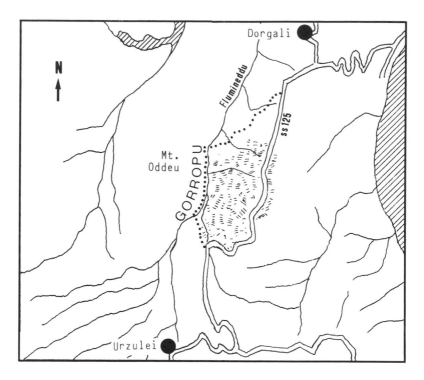

The Gorropu Canyon Adventure

To get to the Gorropu Canyon, take Highway SS 125 from Dorgali towards Urzulei to kilometer mark 178.400. Here you'll find a very small road heading west. Take this for approximately 6 miles (9.5 kilometers) to where the road turns left and begins to head downhill. Soon thereafter you'll see the Flumineddu.

To get to the river, you must lower a rubber boat into the calm water then descend the 49-foot/15-meter rock wall. From here you paddle down the stream. Along the route you will have to climb and descend several cliffs. There are side canyons which can be explored on foot as well as an underground lake and tunnels that intersect the main river.

The canyon venture ends 10 miles (16 kilometers) from where it began, just after passing Mount Oddeu to the left.

The Gorropu Canyon.

There is a well-maintained trail on the right bank which, after a walk of 6.8 miles (11 kilometers), will bring you to kilometer 200.3 of the Highway SS 125.

The time it takes to travel the entire Gorropu Canyon route will depend on the number of persons in your party and their climbing skills. Most adventurers allow 2 days for the trip. Those who enjoy exploring underground caverns and/or unique rock formations, normally add an extra day.

This adventure is best done with a guide or someone who has traveled the canyon previously. A good place to make contact with experts on the canyon, and to pick up gear is the Italian Alpine Club in Cagliari (address in Appendix D).

PART V

BICYCLE TOURING

Coasting the final half-kilometer of Highway 45b into Riva del Garda, Monte Brione came into view as the first rays of sun beamed over its western slopes, giving the entire scene a picture-postcard atmosphere. Snow still lingered on the mountain's upper levels. At lower altitudes, however, the weather was mild and pleasant. The wheels of my Colnago Arabesque, that had been turning steadily for the past 2 hours, came to rest in Piazza Catena, where German, French and a few English tourists were boarding a ferry. It would take them to other tiny towns on Lake Garda, the splendid freshwater lake that joins the Mediterranean regions with the Alps.

Gazing upon the natural beauty of majestic mountains to the east and west, the crystal smooth surface of Lake Garda to the south, and the northern town of Riva del Garda coming to life as if it had suddenly been released from a magical sleep, I realized why so many adventurers are choosing to see Italy by bicycle rather than remaining cooped up in Rome, Venice and Florence.

Though Italy was one of the first countries to host cycling as a competitive sport, it has only been in recent years that enthusiasts have seriously pursued tour biking. Once started, however, the new trend seemed to catch like wildfire, passing from biker to biker. The country's top bicycling magazine, "La Bicicletta", began running 3 tours per issue and special trips quarterly. Touring Club Italiano, well-known publisher of regional maps and guidebooks, has come out with a 167-page practical manual for tour biking, as well as a continuing series of bike itineraries. Today roads throughout Italy are being traveled by athletes pedaling bicycles rigged with panniers, front packs, sleeping bags and one-person nylon tents. Few routes, however, are as crowded with two-wheel traffic as those in the lake country of northern Italy.

Bringing Your Bike Abroad

All international airlines have a free weight allowance of 124 pounds (56 kilograms) which can be distributed between 2 pieces of luggage. In addition one carry-on bag is allowed. If you calculate carefully, your bicycle, clothing, nylon panniers and front pack, foam sleeping bag, cookset, empty containers with tools and miscellaneous articles, a butane stove (purchase cartridges in Italy) and a nylon tent for one person should have a combined weight of far less than the 124-pound limit. To be on the safe side, however, pack heavier items (tools, etc.) into one of the panniers and hand-carry it onto the aircraft. Keep in mind, the lighter you travel the less you will be bogged down when touring.

When going through customs, your bicycle will not have to be declared. New bikes purchased in Italy are normally subject to an import tax upon reentering your native country however—unless it cost less than the duty free limitation. Keep in mind, though, that the duty free limit is a combined total for all taxable items you bring back and not a per-item amount. If your bicycle is of European make, it is best to register it with US customs before leaving or carry a sales receipt as proof that it was not purchased in Europe and, therefore, is not susceptible to customs duties.

Though most airlines prefer bicycles to be boxed, this is not absolutely necessary. A cardboard carton, strengthened with twine once your bicycle has been broken down and placed inside, helps insure proper handling and limits the possibility of damage in transit. But the added weight of packing material must be considered in the overall free weight allowance.

Information on Biking in Italy

There are several organizations which provide information to bikers in Italy. The most popular is the Touring Club Italiano, which also operates the Bicycle Touring Club of Italy (address in Appendix E). Another contact is the Federazione Ciclistica Italia (Via L. Franchetti 2, 00194 Rome, Italy), the governing body for bicycling in Italy. It can provide touring information, addresses of clubs and shops, publications and schedules for cycling competitions.

Biking the Northern Lakes route.

AN EXTENSIVE TOUR OF THE NORTHERN LAKES

The Northern Lakes route begins in Milan, where several international flights arrive daily. Taking in Lakes Maggiore, Lugano, Como, di Endine, Iseo and Garda, the itinerary takes you through a number of typical villages and involves slightly more than 500 miles (805 kilometers) of generally easy cycling through beautiful subtropical scenery and picturesque mountains. Though some of the surrounding peaks reach heights of 6,234 feet (1,900 meters) or more, all roads are situated below 1,017 feet (310 meters). Allowing for a leisurely pace and time to take in attractions, the tour can be completed in 12 to 15 days. Another good feature of the Northern Lakes route is that backtracking is required in only one location, and then only for 15 miles (24 kilometers).

There are many maps that might be used for this biking venture. The most popular are: Michelin 1:200,000 scale, series number 26; Touring Club Italiano 1:500,000 scale, Northern Italy; and the 1:350,000 scale, Lombardia map published by Litografia Artistica Cartografica.

Prior to venturing out, most international travelers find a day in Milan helpful to overcome jet-lag and double-check their gear. From Milan, the route heads east on State Highway 11, to the city of Brescia. This 57-mile/92.3 kilometer excursion normally limbers up muscles and familiarizes touring cyclists with the road signs and conditions of northern Italy.

Noted for its industries and textile plants, Brescia is what one might call a pre-Alpine city, situated at the foot of the Lombard Hills. There are many attractions to be taken in here, including the Piazza della Loggia, the Pinacoteca (picture gallery), the Piazza del Duomo with its 17th-century cathedral and the Roman and Medieval Christian Museums located on Via del Musei in the north-eastern section of the city. It normally takes only half a day to see the sights of Brescia.

Should you run into mechanical difficulties, there are bicy-

The Northern Lakes Route

130

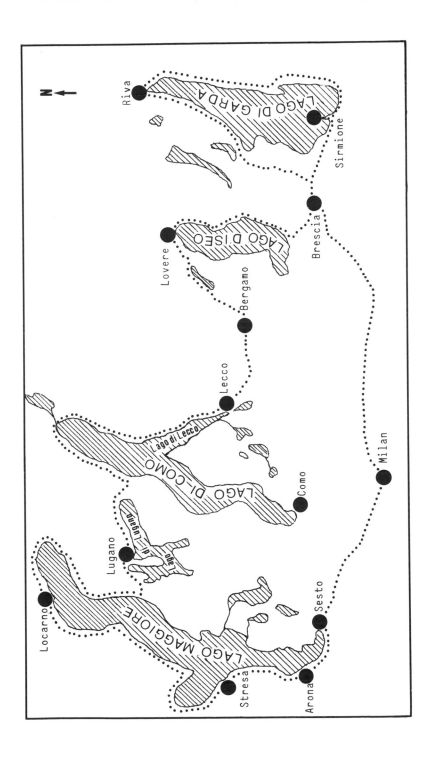

cle shops here that carry parts for major brand bicycles, especially the European makes. One of the better-known outlets is Fratelli Parini, at Via Carini 2/C.

Leaving Brescia, you'll follow Highway 11 east for 6 miles (9.5 kilometers). Here the route continues north on State Road 45b for another 15 miles (24.7 kilometers) to the lakeside resort of Salo.

While Salo contains an interesting 15th century Cathedral with works by Brescia painters Moretto and Romanino, the real attraction here is the beauty of Lake Garda. Along the magnificent shoreline, boat tours of Gardone, Riva, Desenzano and Sirmione run every 3 hours. There are a number of hotels to accommodate visitors in Salo. If you're on a tight budget, you might prefer the camping area at Santa Felice di Benaco, a short distance south on the shore road.

You'll again venture north on 45b when leaving Salo until you reach the northern tip of Lake Garda and the fairytale city of Riva—a distance of 25 miles (41 kilometers).

Located a few miles from the Brenner Pass, Riva boasts a hundred hotels of every class, as well as camping sites. The Tourist Office's Congress Building is the center for cultural and recreational activities, including night clubs and discotheques. The town's nucleus bears traces of a rich historical past. There is a powerful fortress over the lake built by the Venetians. Inside the structure there is a historical museum worth seeing. As a break from pedaling, you might try an alpine hike in the surrounding countryside, perhaps to witness the breathtaking waterfall of Verone 1.9 miles (3 kilometers) north of Riva.

Sirmione, the gem-like peninsula settlement at the southern point of Lake Garda is the next stop on your route. To get here from Riva you'll pass through stunning mountain scenery as you head south for 40 miles (64.5 kilometers) on State Highway 249 to the town of Peschiera. Here you turn north-west on Highway 11 to Colombare and up the peninsula to Sirmione.

This tiny peninsula runs in a south-to-north direction for almost 2 miles (3 kilometers), covering an area of only 247 acres. But you will find almost every imaginable vacation comfort here—from bars and discotheques, to ancient art and historical remains.

Of all the resorts on Lake Garda, Sirmione is perhaps the most appealing. A number of factors contribute to its fame: the beauty of the landscape; the remains of the magnificent Roman villa, "Le Grotte di Catullo"; the Scaligero Castle; fascinating medieval architecture; clean beaches; and the spring known as "La Boiola" that supplies water to several thermal baths.

Like most of the region's cities, Sirmione contains an array of accommodation facilities from modern and elegant hotels to relatively inexpensive campsites.

Leaving Lake Garda and its enchanting villages is often hard to do. But there is still much to cover and many sights to be seen. The first stage on your continued journey is to travel 24 miles (38 kilometers) west on State Highway 11 back to Brescia. Depending on what time you arrive, you might pass through the city, staying on Highway 11 for another 3.7 miles (6 kilometers) where you'll turn north-west on Highway 469 to Lake Iseo and the city which bears the same name.

Unlike Lake Garda, Lake Iseo does not boast luxurious villas or hundreds of first-class hotels. What this 15.5-mile 25-kilometer stretch of fresh water does offer is genuine hospitality and undisturbed nature along shores abundant with olive trees and bordered by majestic mountains and charming villages.

There is little to see from a historical standpoint in the town of Iseo, other than the "Pieve"—a Romanesque church in the main square with a 13th century campanile. It does, however, offer a good camping facility and a friendly, peaceful atmosphere.

Continuing north on Route 469 along the lake shore you'll pass through several small villages until you reach the city of Lovere, 17 miles (28 kilometers) from Iseo. This is another good camping area, situated on the lake. The Tadini Museum is here with works by Giovanni Bellini and Il Parmigianino, in addition to collections of weapons, porcelain and sculptures by Canova.

You'll encounter a number of charming places along the northern Italy route. Unless you have plenty of time, though—more than 2 weeks—it is best to forge on ahead if you are to complete the tour.

Since there is some distance to cover after leaving Lovere, it is best to begin early, picking up Highway 42 as you head south. This road takes you along the Cavallina mountain range, past the limpid waters of Lake di Endine and into the twin city of Bergamo, a total distance of 25 miles (41 kilometers). Here you have the option of remaining to take in the city's attractions (actually it is two cities under one name) or continuing to Lecco, your next overnight stop, on the borders of Lakes Garlate and Lecco.

There is much to see in Bergamo if time allows: the 16th century Venetian architecture; the splendid Piazza Vecchia; the Baptistry; the Colleoni Chapel; and the Church of Santa Maria Maggiore, with its tapestries and superb 16th century panels. All of these are found in the "upper" town of Bergamo. In the "lower" town, you'll discover the Carrara Academy filled with works of famous Italian artists. Also in the lower town is the picturesque Via Pigolo.

The distance from Bergamo to Lecco is 20.5 miles (33 kilometers) via Highway 342. An industrial town, Lecco is the gateway to Lake Como, which extends to the north for 29.8 miles (48 kilometers). In fact, the two lakes that this city divides—Garlate and Lecco—are merely the eastern extremity of Lake Como.

This region is abundant with olive groves, mulberries, chestnuts, walnuts and fig trees, not to mention the oleanders that decorate the shoreline. In this mountainous setting, Lecco offers visitors not only natural beauty, but excellent accommodations at reasonable prices.

In one day's time you should be able to travel from Lecco, up Highway 36, around the northern tip of Lake Como and come down the western shore on Highway 34. This 46-mile/74.7-kilometer ride ranges from leisurely biking to medium inclines. In most cases, though, the scenery will keep your mind off the physical efforts required in this stretch of the trip.

The next stop is Menaggio, one of the smallest, but best

equipped tourist centers on Lake Como. Here you will find an array of hotels, campsites, beaches and restaurants in addition to facilities—if you have energy—for tennis, water skiing, windsurfing and golf.

While in this Eden-like resort, where gardens abound, do take advantage of the delicate gustatory delights that are brought in daily from the 1,476-foot (450-meter) depths of Lake Como and featured in local restaurants. Trout, eel and the shad-like "agoni" are all served to perfection.

A 4-hour boat tour of the take can be taken from Menaggio. The steamer makes 2 trips daily, also docking in the lake-side towns of Colico, Como, Argego and Bellagio to take on and off-load passengers.

On the next leg of your journey, be sure you have easy access to your passport. For you'll now take Highway 340 west (it also runs north and south) towards Lugano, Switzerland. This is not a long trip—20 miles (32.6 kilometers)—but it is one of extreme beauty as you travel the Lake Lugano coast. This 22-mile/35-kilometer lake lies mostly in Swiss territory and is encompassed by steep Alpine slopes peppered with wild olive trees.

A day in Lugano is highly recommended. The typical mountain town contains a delightful Municipal Park with colorful gardens along the water's edge, the Cathedral of San Lorenzo, the church of Santa Martia degli Angioli, the 17th century Villa Favorita with its private picture collection that includes works by Van Dyck, Rubens, Caravaggio and others. In the surroundings of Lugano are the San Salvatore and Bre Mountains, where short hikes result in views that one finds only in the Alps.

Keep in mind that in Lugano you'll be spending Swiss francs, not Italian lira.

Fourteen miles (23 kilometers) west of this Swiss town on Highway 24, you'll come to Luino, an attractive resort on Lake Maggiore. Just before reaching Luino, you'll re-enter Italy.

Like the other lakes you have seen in your travels, Lake Maggiore can be toured by boat. The tour takes about 4 hours. Surrounding tropical vegetation, varied landscape and friendly inhabitants make this Italy's most famous lake. In

Lake Maggiore, along the Northern Lakes route.

the central part of the lake the Borromean Islands sit like tiny gems, offering historical, artistic and natural delights to all who visit.

Most touring cyclists find pleasant accommodations 5 minutes north of Luino, in the village of Maccagno. Here, encompassed by nature's pleasures, is one of Lake Maggiore's largest campsites.

Moving on, you head north along Highway 394 into the Alps and, again, Switzerland. Your destination this time is the Lake Maggiore haven of Locarno, a town of 17,000 inhabitants.

As in Brescia and many of the cities you have passed through, there are bicycle shops here offering assistance, parts and plenty of friendly conversation on Italian bicycling.

In addition to the city's colorful gardens, and an 18 hole golf course, there are the 15th century Visconti Castle and small museum. Most tourists also delight in visiting the church of the Madonna del Sasso, situated on a summit at 1,263 feet

(385 meters). Another attraction is the view from the high Cimetta peak which can easily be reached by cable car.

Biking down the western coast of Lake Maggiore on Route 34 and changing to Route 33 at Fondo Toce, you'll enter the town of Stresa after traveling exactly 35.4 miles (57 kilometers).

This is a delightful town and an excellent base for excursions on Lake Maggiore or into the neighboring mountains. The park of the Villa Pallavicino is one place you should not miss. It contains not only an array of flower gardens, but a host of wild animals such as deer, lamas, ostriches and pheasants. For panoramic views of the Po Plains, the lakes and the Alps, a venture to the Mottarone summit (4,921 feet/1,500 meters) is recommended. For those who have a fear of heights, the Giardino Alpini, about half-way up , also offers an excellent view.

The friendly people at the Tourist Office in the city's Congress Building can provide you with details of lake tours as well as local events and facilities.

With Stresa, your tour of Italy's most beautiful lakes is nearly complete. The final excursion takes you 18 miles (29 kilometers) along Highway 33, around the southern tip of Lake Maggiore to the little town of Sesto Calende.

From here you may either catch one of the daily trains to Milan or, if time allows, continue along Route 33 for an additional 33.8 miles (54.5 kilometers) to where your tour began.

TOURING UMBRIA

Bicycle touring through Umbria offers a world of ancient charm; the reserved beauty of the landscape, the human dimension of everything you encounter, and the picturesque villages all recall the simple life of the past. Also found here is a special way of getting close to nature—it becomes easy to understand St. Francis and his religion based on a love of the simple life. The Franciscan simplicity is really a reflection of the simple Umbrian world.

Situated in the middle of the Italian peninsula, Umbria is often referred to as the "heart" of the country. One of the few regions without coastal areas, Umbria is crossed by the Apennines sloping into gentle hills which vary and soften the countryside.

Its towns, artistic gems which have maintained much of their original charm, include Perugia, Gubbio, Spoleto, Todi, Orvieto, Assisi, Spello, Trevi, Cascia, Norcia and many others. Most are of medieval origin, set in dominating positions and enclosed by towering walls.

But Umbria is above all its people, whose affable modesty comes from a tradition in the remote past.

The Umbria route is 118 miles (191 kilometers) round-trip and can easily be covered in 4–5 days. This includes time to take in local attractions. It begins in Perugia, a city known for its great history, beauty and art. Leaving Perugia, go north-

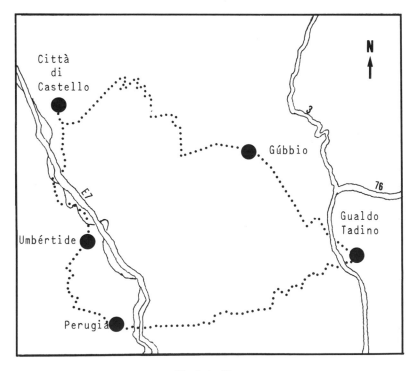

Umbria Tour

west along Corso Garibaldi and Via Monte Ripido. It is a panoramic route amidst hills and tiny villages. A road rises on the right from the Tiber Valley to the Abbey of St. Salvatore di Monte Corona—home of the Camaldolesi Coronesi Order, founded by St. Romualdo in 1008.

The city of Umbertide is also in the Tiber Valley and the art of pottery-making is practiced there as it has been for centuries. Outstanding is the 1651 church of Sta. Croce with a painting by Signorelli. The Castle of Montalto and magnificent Castle of Civitella Ranieri (15th–16th centuries) are also nearby.

Continue north along Highway 3b, through Montecastelli and on to Città di Castello. There are a number of things to see in this town, which dates to the Roman period, including the Gothic palace of the Podestà, the Gothic Communal Palace, the Bishop's Palace, and the 11th century cathedral. There are also several churches rich in art and history.

On the southern side of the city, to the left of Highway 219, there is a little-used road which, after a long twisting stretch reaches the tiny village of Pietralunga where the ruins of a fortress can be visited. Return now to Highway 219 and continue your excursion to Gúbbio, an ancient Umbrian town full of history, art and tradition. Some of the attractions most visitors enjoy in Gúbbio are: the Old Town around Piazza della Signoria; the Palace of the Consuls; the Ducal Palace; the Roman theater; the cathedral and the church of St. Francis.

From Gúbbio, Highway 219 leads to Branca, a village surrounded by lovely countryside. Continue on 219, out of the city, turning left towards Fossato di Vico. After 1.9 miles (3 kilometers), turn right and go into Gualdo Tadino.

Gualdo Tadino is one of Italy's most famous centers for production of artistic pottery highlighted with rich polychrome and metallic reflections. During July and August the International Pottery Exhibition and Competition is held here. In addition, the city has a 13th century cathedral which, today, houses the rich Communal Art Gallery.

From Gualdo Tadino it's a 29-mile/47-kilometer journey along Highway 318 to Perugia, where the Umbria tour began.

Umbria in Springtime.

THE RUIN ROUTE

This route, in southern Italy, covers some of the country's most famous ruins, beginning with the ancient city of Cumae and ending at the archeological zone of Paestum. Along the 71-mile 115-kilometer route that connects these two pre-Roman cities are the famed Baths of Baiae, the Serapeum at Pozzuoli, the beautiful remains of the town of Ercolano, and the world-renowned Pompeii.

The entire coastal region from Cumae to Paestum was once inhabited by Greek refugees. As these colonies began to expand, cities such as Naples, Pompeii, Sorrento and Salerno were established. Although the ancient Greek people held off both land and sea invasions for many centuries, by the time of the Roman Empire, the original colonies had either been abandoned or joined the new empire willingly. But the culture that was established under the pattern of ancient Athens became the blueprint for the new Roman life-style.

Because the ruin route passes through many populated areas, where streets are congested and one can easily become lost, some of the travel is best done by train. In fact, you can take this tour equally well on a bicycle or as a hiking adventure.

The ruin route begins 12 miles (20 kilometers) outside the heart of Naples at the Acropolis of Cumae. To get here, take the Via Domitiana (SS 7) west to kilometer mark 50. Here, turn left onto Via Vecchia Cuma. Take it for 1.5 miles (2.5 kilometers) and the ancient city will be visible on your right. There are also signs pointing the way.

Cumae is the oldest archaeological site in Italy; the town was founded in the 8th century B.C. by a group of Greek colonists. The Acropolis still has its 5th century B.C. walls, and is comprised of the Temple of Apollo, the Temple of Jupiter, the famous Grotto of the Sibilla (mentioned by Virgil in the Aeneid), the Roman crypt, the remains of an impressive thermal bath system and the Amphitheater. There are also many tombs of the Greek and Roman periods.

According to tradition, the Grotto of the Sibilla or Sibyl was utilized by a cult of women who could communicate with the Gods. The head of the group was the Sibyl, who was said to sit in the hollowed out section at the end of the long corridor and foretell the future. Ancient scrolls tell of Roman Emperors journeying to Cumae to ask her advice on such matters as war, laws and political alliances.

Upon leaving Cumae, turn right onto Via Cuma (the spelling of the "modern" town of Cuma is without the "e" ending). This will take you to the village of Fusaro, 2 miles (3.5 kilometers) down the road. There are a couple of good restaurants in the town, but for a quick eat-and-run meal, try the "salumeria" to the left as you pass along the Via Cuma. This tiny "general store" prepares one of the best Italian sandwiches in the area. Continuing on, go over the railroad tracks and turn left, following the sign to Naples. A short distance ahead, on your right, you will see a dome-shaped structure. This is your next stop—the Parco Archaeologia di Baia.

The Roman baths of Baia are among the most interesting ruins in the world. They were very popular with the Romans

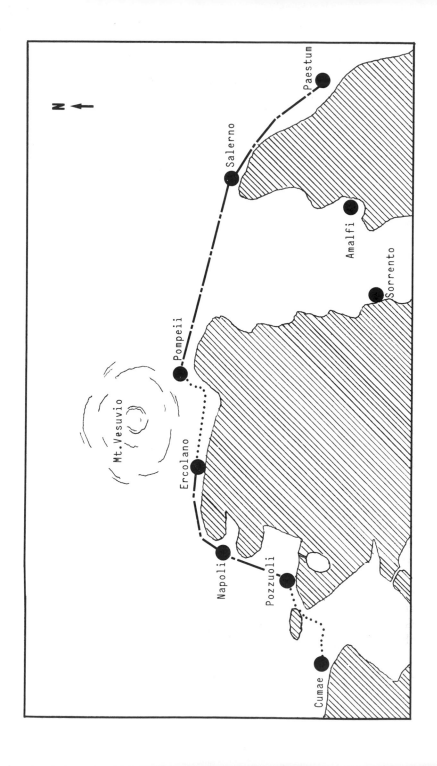

N

Paestum

Salerno

Amalfi

Sorrento

Pompeii

Mt.Vesuvio

Ercolano

Napoli

Pozzuoli

Cumae

during the Imperial Age and were surrounded by elegant villas. The excavations have uncovered remains of the once-luxurious Imperial Palace, including the Baths of Jasardra, the Baths of Mercury, the Baths of Venus and the Temple of Diana. Further excavations in the sea along the coast of Baia, which began in 1979, have disclosed the ruins of streets and buildings from still earlier periods.

From the baths of Baia, continue along through Archo Felice and into the historical town of Pozzuoli. This is the largest settlement in the Campi Flegrei (Phlegrean Fields) area west of Naples. A pleasant, colorful maritime town overlooking an attractive bay, Pozzuoli was a busy trading and commercial center in Roman times, and there are still some remains of that period. The major sites are the Serapeo, an ancient Flavian market place, still well preserved in spite of the sinking of the land, which has menaced the whole Phlegrean Fields area for many centuries; the Flavian Ampitheater (the third largest in Italy), famous for its large underground caverns and, in the immediate vicinity, the Solfatara. This is one of the most impressive volcanic phenomena known, an ancient crater with fumaroles, carbon dioxide, mineral water springs and jets of volcanic mud whose temperature reaches 160° C (320° F).

Pozzuoli is a good place to stop for the evening. There are hotels in the area as well as two campsites: one at the Solfatara; the other (Camping Averno) at kilometer 55 of the Via Domitiana.

If you spend the night in Pozzuoli, you might want to slip down to the port area before moving on to the next stop. Each morning between 5 and 9 a.m. local fishermen gather to sell their catch. You will see everything from tuna to balloon fish; and the colorful townsfolk that this event attracts will make it well worth your effort.

The next location on the ruin route is some distance away, through many little towns. So as not to waste time, from Pozzuoli take the local train to the main station in Naples' Piazza Garibaldi. On the first floor of the train station you will find the Circumvesuviana. This train travels to Ercolano, Mount

The Ruin Route

143

Vesuvius, Pompeii and Sorrento. From 4 a.m. to 4 p.m. trains run about every 45 minutes. You can also take the Naples-Ercolano bus. You will find it in front of the train station—either number 157 or 159. The ride takes about 20 minutes. Traveling with a bicycle, however, it is easier to take a train.

Ercolano is the next stop on this excursion, the site of ancient Herculaneum. It is a small town, and it is not difficult to find the ruins—there are signs on every other corner. In fact, most of the buses, and the train, stop right outside the excavation site.

Unlike its sister city, Pompeii, when the eruption of Vesuvius covered Ercolano it preserved rather than burned the town. This was one of the most elegant Roman towns during its period. Most of the residential center was dotted with rich villas that overlooked the beautiful bay.

Excavations in Ercolano first began in 1738 under the order of Charles III of Bourbon. Because of the unusual mixture of volcanic mud and lava, the archaeologists discovered that many delicate objects had been preserved. You will notice some of these finds as you walk along the ancient Corso Ercolano.

Having whetted your appetite for ruins, you can now tackle the largest such site Italy has to offer—Pompeii. Outside the ruins at Ercolano there are signs indicating the way to Pompeii. Following these, it is very easy to find the city. Once you are in Pompeii the ruins seem to jump out wherever you look. Actually, you enter the town near the first entrance to the archaeological site.

Because it takes some time to visit the ruins, it is best to find a place to stay for the night and visit the modern city of Pompeii—leaving the ruins for the next day. The best, and closest, place for those with a tent is the campsite just across the street from the ruins. Those looking for a little more comfort will find an array of hotels in the vicinity.

Visiting the ruins of Pompeii is like stepping back in time. The eruption of Vesuvius in 79 A.D. buried this flourishing commercial center, with 20,000 inhabitants, under a deep mantle of pebbles, mud and ash. In the 17th century, some of its remains were discovered by chance and in 1754 the first systematic excavations began. However it was only in the last two centuries that excavations have been conducted along rational and scientific lines. These have now brought to light most of the ancient city dwellings.

Once you are oriented, like most visitors you will probably be fascinated by the imposing public structures such as the Forum, the many temples, thermal baths, theaters and amphitheaters; by the variety of houses and shops; and by the unique wall paintings, mosaics and statues. Some of the places you should not miss are the House of Vetti—for its mosaics and pornographic history—the House of the Faun, the Stabian Baths, the Gladiator School and the Basilica.

If you are covering the ruin route during the summer months, you might be interested in knowing that the ancient theater of Pompeii is still used in July, August and September. A performance is given every evening, beginning at dusk.

After a day of walking, few have the energy or desire to ride off to Paestum, which is the next stop. Most prefer to spend another night in Pompeii and get an early start. The ruin route can be covered in 4–6 days. If you are pushed for time, you might take the train to Paestum from Pompeii—it departs at 5 a.m. and 2:55 p.m. The later train will allow you to visit any sites you overlooked in the ruins the previous day.

Those continuing by bicycle should take SS 18 heading west out of Pompeii. Staying on this highway for 37 miles (60 kilometers), passing through Salerno and Battipaglia, you will reach Paestum.

The city of Paestum was originally a Greek colony founded in the 7th century B.C. under the name Poseidonia. During the Greek and Roman periods the city grew and flourished through import and trade. In the Middle Ages, however, the coast line began to sink, causing the Salso River near Paestum to silt up. This turned the area into a backwater. As a result of this and the increasing raids on the city all inhabitants gradually departed. Thus, Paestum remained uninhabited and forgotten until early in the 18th century. The main excavations here are the Basilica, Temple of Neptune, Forum and Temple of Ceres. The 3 temples that face the entrance are in the Doric style that was popular with the Greeks in 450 B.C. Near the second set of temples, to your right as you enter, is the main

Paestum, last stop on the ruin route.

town—now leveled to a height of 3 feet (1 meter). This is still, however, an interesting zone to visit.

The museum, situated across the street from the excavations, contains many of the city's remains. Most impressive are the huge mosaics that depict scenes of Greek life around the town swimming pool and battles against local invaders.

Paestum brings you to the end of the ruin route. You have covered some of the finest remains of Greek and Roman culture to be found anywhere in the world—something that will stay with you for a long time to come.

TRAVELING THE VIA APPIA

The Via Appia covers much of Italy, from Rome to Brindisi. It runs for 365 miles (587 kilometers) and should be traveled at a leisurely pace, allowing time to take in local attractions. Most cyclers allow a couple of weeks for this extensive excursion. There are many hotels, campsites and restaurants along the way; therefore, finding accommodations for the night should be no problem.

Beyond the grand arena known as the Colosseum, amid the remnants of the Forum, is a section from the base of the Milliarium Aureum, the "golden milestone." Erected in 20 B.C. by Augustus, the first emperor, the gilded bronze column listed the mileage between Rome and her principal cities.

By the beginning of the 2nd century A.D. hundreds of roads led to Rome. No route achieved the lasting fame, however, of the Via Appia whose stones have felt the tread of Hannibal and St. Paul, Charlemagne, Lord Byron and Mark Twain.

Along the cobblestones of the ancient Appian Way history has unfolded. It was here, in 71 B.C., that 6,000 rebellious slaves were crucified. Led by gladiator Spartacus, the slaves had fought the Romans for nearly 3 years. Upon their capture, the rebels were strung side-by-side along the 132-mile/212 kilometer route between Rome and Capua, where they were left to rot.

The Appian Way offers both historical and natural attractions.

Rich Romans attempted to gain immortality by constructing tombs along the Appia so passing travelers could read their names.

Poor Christians too found a home for their dead on the Appia. Unlike the wealthy Romans, however, they had to content themselves with cramming hundreds of thousands of their dead into tiered coffinlike niches cut into rock catacombs underground.

Life along the ancient Appian Way was not all tragic nor morbid. Towns grew and prospered. The pulse of life throbbed in the villages that lined the road, as the plunder of the empire poured into southern ports and moved overland to Rome. The road also opened a marketplace for small vendors and sidewalk shops.

Today, while much has changed, much has remained basically the same along Via Appia. One can still find vendors pushing carts and chanting at the top of their lungs to lure potential clients. Though tiny Fiats and zigzagging motorbikes have replaced the parade of chariots and horsemen, horse-drawn farm wagons are still occasionally seen. Lovers continue to find romance in a peaceful carriage ride along the Appia, as did the youth of antiquity. And now, as then, the narrow two-lane Appia barely accommodates the heavy traffic. Unlike Julius Caesar, who banned most daytime wheeled traffic in 45 B.C.—creating clamorous and often sleepless nights—today's Italians have accepted the congestion and resulting "free-for-all" driving conditions.

Despite its defects, the Appian Way is a rare treat for touring bicyclers, particularly those with a passion for history and ancient lifestyles.

Via Appia was the first and most important "consular road" built by the Romans. Rightly called "regina viarum" (queen of roads), it was begun in 312 B.C., under the order of Appius Claudius, to establish a direct and fast means of communication between Rome and Capua. It was planned in an extraordinarily "modern" manner, avoiding larger towns that could be connected to the main artery by secondary roads. The road went straight to its final destination. Its tracking required remarkable engineering skill to overcome several natural obstacles. At a time when elaborate road systems were unknown, the Romans scaled mountains, filled swamps, and crossed plains with highways as straight as a stretched ribbon.

Via Appia was paved with large slabs of variable shaped basaltic stone—which are still used for repairing certain sections of the road. The standard width was 14 roman feet (about 4.15 meters), enough to allow two carts to pass at the same time. At the sides of the road were sidewalks of tamped earth, each at least 5 feet (1.5 meters) wide and delimited by curbstones. Every 7–9 miles (11–14 kilometers) in areas of heavy traffic and every 10–12 miles (16–19 kilometers) in light-traffic zones, horse changing posts were established, as well as rest houses and inns for voyagers. Many of these posts still exist, though their function is now that of road maintenance.

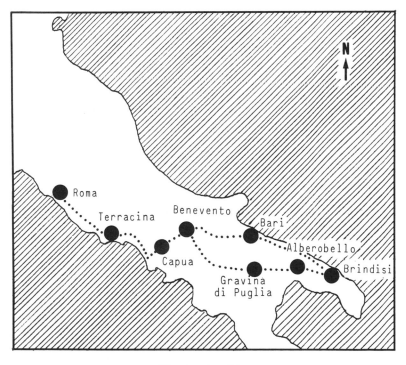

The Appian Way

The first segment of Via Appia—Rome to Terracina—consists of a 56-mile/90-kilometer straightaway. The last 17 miles (28 kilometers) of this segment were originally flanked by a drainage canal, allowing the journey to be made by boat as well as by horse or cart. Past Terracina, the road bent through a mountain pass towards the village of Fondi. It then touched Formiae (now Formia), Minturnae (Minturno) and Sinuessa (the modern town of Mondragone) before reaching Casilinum (today Capua) on the Volturno river, and from there reached ancient Capua (now called Santa Maria Capua Vetere). The total distance was 132 miles (212 kilometers) and could normally be covered in 5 to 6 days.

The Via Appia was then prolonged: first to Benevento, then beyond the Apennine Mountains to Venosa and later to Taranto. Finally, in the early 2nd century B.C., it was lengthened as far as the Adriatic port of Brindisi, the so-called gateway to the east. In A.D. 109, the Benevento-Brindisi route closed, and the shorter, easier Via Appia Traiana route was created which crossed the entire Puglia region, touching the towns of Troia, Ordona, Canosa, Ruvo, Bari and Egnazia. The new road allowed travelers to venture from Rome to Brindisi in 10 or 15 days, covering a total distance of 365 miles (587 kilometers).

Today, thousands of visitors each year enjoy a journey into Italy's past as they travel this route which has carried so many personalities and seen so much history. What most travelers actually follow is a "third" branch of the Appia, SS (State Highway) 7, the Appia Nuovo. This runs atop the Antica, or near it, to just beyond Benevento. Here it veers off, leaving the Appian track until near Taranto.

Beginning in Rome, the Appian Way is a haunt of history and beauty because of the fragmented monuments left along it and the unique and solemn landscape it runs through. One segment of the road, about a mile long, contains no fewer than 50 historical monuments. This section runs from Rome's Porta San Sebastiano, a gate through the Aurelian Wall constructed in the second half of the 3rd century A.D. as Porta Appia. The

Along the Appian Way.

little church of "Domine quo Vadis" is situated about half a mile from the gate; here according to tradition, Jesus appeared to St. Peter, who was running away from Rome. Further on there are the Catacombs of St. Callixtus, the Jewish Catacombs, the Basilica of St. Sebastian and catacombs of the same name, the tomb of Romulus, the remains of the Circus of Maxentius, the tomb of Cecilia Metella, the Villa dei Quintili, and the so-called "Casal Rotondo" mausoleum, among others.

Leaving Rome, you pass through Cisterna di Latina, then Mesa, and arrive in Terracina, a town of 33,500 inhabitants. On the 748-foot/228-meter summit of Monti Ausoni, overlooking this modern seaside resort, sits a vast horizontal structure of limestone and marble, topped by arches. It is the foundation of an ancient temple. Though signs indicate the Temple of Zeus, there is debate as to whether or not the monument was in reality built for the goddess Venus.

It is said that the Appia originally passed over the summit in Terracina, requiring both time and effort for travelers. Trajan, therefore, cut a 118-foot/36-meter route through the cliffs allowing an easy passage.

The city maintains an excellent Archaeological Museum containing Greek and Roman statues and fragments from local excavations.

From Terracina, it is a beautiful coastal drive to Sperlonga, where a modern museum has been erected to display the works uncovered during excavation of a seaside estate believed to have been owned by Emperor Tiberius. Among the finds are the fragments of a larger-than-life marble Cyclops Polyphemus being attacked by Odysseus (Ulysses to the Romans). Attributed to the three Rhodian sculptors who produced the famed Laöcoön group in the Vatican, the masterpiece was found within the Grotto of Tiberius. This grotto, along with the remnants of the ancient city, can be visited by walking from the museum a short distance to the sea.

Leaving Sperlonga, Via Appia Nuovo continues along the coast, taking in cities such as Gaeta and Formia before coming to the remains of ancient Minturnae, just south of modern Minturno. This was a prosperous Roman city that reached its height during the 2nd century A.D. Remarkably preserved original stones of the Appia run through the ruins, past broken columns of a once grand portico. The city's theater, now restored, stages classical plays in summer.

Not far away are the remains of the aqueduct which serviced the city. About 328 feet (100 meters) from the ancient city, Appia passes over the River Garigliano which was called the Lirisi in antiquity. To the right are the statue foundations from the original bridge crossing.

Via Appia next turns west towards Capua which in Roman times was called Casilinum. The original site of the town is today located at Santa Maria Capua Vetere. It was here that Hannibal held off the Romans, by blocking the Via Appia. In 216 B.C. Hannibal was finally defeated here.

A city of much history, Santa Maria's highlight is the evocative remains of an amphitheater built by emperor Hadrian. In 73 B.C., Spartacus died here. Before his debut in the arena, however, he began the Slave War which eventually set nearly 100,000 runaway slaves against the Romans. After the death of Spartacus, the rebels were soon captured and strung out to die a slow and painful death along the Appia.

From here the Appia extends to Benevento, today a modern city of 59,000 inhabitants. In honor of Trajan, the Romans constructed a 49-foot/15-meter triumphal arch across the Via Appia in this location—an arch which still stands. A school for gladiators was established here in ancient times. Many of the works of art that adorned that school can now be seen in the city's Museo del Sannio.

Also in Benevento are the remains of a Roman Theater, built in the reign of Hadrian and enlarged by Caracalla to accommodate 20,000 spectators.

From Benevento you have the option of continuing along the Via Appia to the south-west, or taking Via Appia Traiana to the west and eventually south. Many travelers continue their route on the original road and return via the Traiana. Whatever the itinerary, you will eventually arrive in Brindisi. Along the way, however, you will pass through a series of small towns, each with its historical link to the Appia and its own attractions.

Excavation suggests that the town the Greeks called Sidion

was succeeded by the Romans' Silvium, mentioned as an Appia stop by ancient travelers. Today this site is the town of Gravina di Puglia and may conceal the ruins of the Roman settlement beneath its old section.

Not far off the Appia Traiana is the town of Alberobello, where for centuries villagers have constructed beehive homes called "trulli". The reason for these strange and beautiful structures is that the steep limestone-slab roofs direct the infrequent rainwater to underground cisterns. Their thick whitewashed walls insure cool shelter during the hot, Mediterranean summers.

Another place along the Traiana route not to be overlooked is the Adriatic port of Egnazia. The walled Acropolis and the town proper lie respectively on the east and west sides of the highway. Among other attractions here are a Roman Forum paved with large stone blocks and flanked by remains of a colonnaded portico, an ancient basilica, what is believed to be an amphitheater, and the ruins of an early-Christian basilica.

The "trulli" homes of Alberobello, a short distance off the ruin route.

While all roads supposedly lead to Rome, most visitors find that Via Appia eventually leads to Brindisi, a city which joined the Roman Empire in the 3rd century B.C. The city flourished under Roman rule, becoming a major naval base for the Second Punic War. Here, crusades began and ended. Here, triumphant Romans returning home with the spoils of war began their cross-country journey by foot, hoof, cart, and litter; a journey that, according to a gilded bronze column located in the Roman Forum, covered more than 365 miles (587 kilometers) along the Appian Way.

BIKING THROUGH SARDINIA

One of the best ways to get to know Sardinia is by bicycle. The following itineraries have been designed to give you an overall view of this splendid island: the real, everyday Sardinia. They will allow you to acquire a closer knowledge of the people, traditions, archaeology, crafts, nature and gastronomy.

Each of the following routes covers a distance of approximately 125 miles (200 kilometers) and can be covered in a few days. The itineraries cover various areas of the island—north, south, east, west—and incorporate numerous points of interest. For those who would like to extend their time and cover Sardinia completely, a booklet of 20 itineraries is available by writing the regional tourist board (address in Appendix C).

THE SOUTHERN ROUTE

The southern route begins in Santa Margherita di Pula, a well-known holiday resort on the south-west coast of the Gulf of Cagliari. Here there are hotels, tourist villages and many villas and bungalows in the thick pine woods.

Following the SS 195, turn off after 5 miles (8 kilometers) at the sign for the archaeological area at Nora. From a 16th century tower that stood guard against Saracen invaders, the visitor can admire the important remains of the town. A commercial port founded by the Phoenicians and later taken

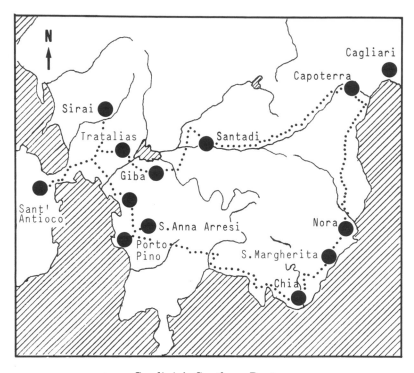

Sardinia's Southern Route

over by the Romans, Nora declined and eventually disappeared around the 3rd century A.D.

Back on SS 195 you come to the fork in the road for Capoterra, pass through this center and take the road for Santadi. The road goes through an extremely wild countryside among oak woods, ravines and Mediterranean maquis including all types of plants from lentisks to myrtle and arbutus. In winter the hills are red with arbutus berries and the sweet-flavored black or white myrtle berries fill the air with their perfume.

In spring the maquis is covered with an incredible number of flowers. After the first autumn rains a plentiful crop of tasty mushrooms comes up. Wild boar live in the woods along with deer, of which there is a strain found only in these parts. Many

The Sardinia countryside.

species of birds, both permanent and migratory, are to be found in these hills along the river Gutturu Mannu as far as Santadi.

Once you have reached the plain of Palmas, take the SS 293, turn south and you come to the village of Giba. Now leave the main road and head for Tratalias.

In this village, close to the artificial lake of Monte Pranu, stands a Romanesque church, Santa Maria, whose extraordinarily pure architecture is reminiscent of Tuscan Romanesque, with some Gothic influence. The church dates to the 12th century.

Follow the SS 126 now, heading for Sirai, turn off at the sign and climb up onto the plateau where a Carthaginian settlement has recently been brought to light. This is evidence for the importance of Sardinia, at least the southern part of the island, in the commercial, political and military system of Carthage. This site is well worth visiting.

Going back towards San Giovanni Suergiu, take the road and the causeway that link the island of Sant'Antioco to the mainland. It appears that the Carthaginians built a causeway at this point, and it is certain that the Romans reinforced it and built a bridge that can still be seen today.

After the harbor you come to Sant'Antioco, a town rich in history. Today it is a well-known seaside resort, with traces of the ancient civilizations that dominated the area. In the excavation area there is an interesting museum containing the objects found during various excavations.

Calasetta is the port from which ferry boats leave Sant'Antioco for Carloforte.

Returning over the causeway, go back to San Giovanni Suergiu and take the SS 195 as far as Villarios, then turn onto the secondary road that leads to the attractive town of Porto Pino with its pine woods and its lagoon full of fish. After a visit here, go back to SS 195 to Sant'Anna Arresi. After 6 miles (10 kilometers), turn onto the spectacular coast road that leads to Chia and rejoins SS 195 a few miles from Santa Margherita. The road follows the scenic route past high cliffs plunging down into the sea, rugged promontories, and beaches of very fine sand. It leads from Porto Teulada to Capo Malfatano, Capo

Spartivento and Chia, where the great sand dunes, studded with juniper bushes, merge with the luxuriant Mediterranean maquis.

A few traces of the ancient Carthaginian settlement of Bithnia can be seen on the beach at Chia, overlooked by an old 16th century watch-tower.

The last part of the journey is through wild scenery between the sea and the harsh rocky hills all the way to Santa Margherita di Pula.

THE WESTERN ROUTE

The western route begins in Oristano, the chief town of the province of the same name. Rich in history, Oristano has the

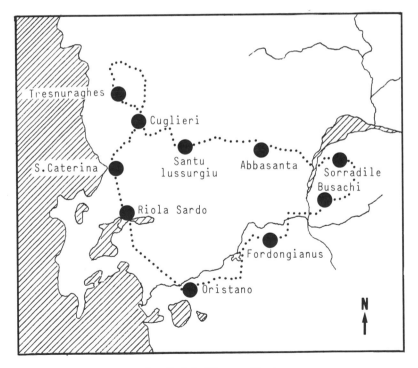

Sardinia's Western Route

character of a farming and commercial center. Among its famous monuments are the Tower of San Cristoforo, better known as the "Tower of Mariano," and the 16th century palace which tradition would have us believe was the home of the famous ruler Eleonora d'Arborea, although she in fact lived many years before it was even built.

In its strategic position on the fertile alluvial plain of the River Tirso, crowned by the hills of Ferru and Arci and the plateau of Abbasanta, between the sea and Lake Omodeo, Oristano is the product of various civilizations: the pastoral, the peasant and the fishing worlds.

Taking the SS 388 through an agricultural countryside of rice-fields, you come to Simaxis and then, by way of the typical villages of Ollastra Simaxis and Villanova Truschedu, you reach Fordongianus. Just before reaching the town, you might want to stop and admire the pure Romanesque style of the little country church of Santu Lussurgiu.

Fordongianus was an important military center for the Romans. A witness of its past are the large Roman baths which made use of the springs of radioactive salt water that still flow at a temperature of over 60° C (140° F) along the banks of the river Tirso.

Cross the bridge over the Tirso and follow the SS 388 through a landscape of high hills, rich with vineyards and oak woods, to Busachi. Known as the longest village in Sardinia because it follows the line of the main road with very little development beyond the road, Busachi is one of the most faithful towns to its own tradition. It is not unusual to find old women sitting outside homes embroidering in their costumes, while here and there along the road a saffron-yellow cloth will remind you that on Sardinia yellow is the color of mourning.

Continuing along Route 388 for another 3 miles (5 kilometers), you turn off for Neoneli and Nughedu Santa Vittoria through scenery that becomes increasingly wild with thick woods and little gorges. At Nughedu Santa Vittoria you go down towards Sorradile, with a beautiful view of Lake Omodeo below. Cross the bridge at Tadasuni, the narrowest point of this artificial lake which was created in 1920 by the biggest dam in Europe. Then go up to the village of Tadasuni. From Tadasuni you begin the climb towards Zuri.

Before flooding the valley to create Lake Omodeo, the Romanesque church of San Pietro was dismantled stone by stone and rebuilt at Zuri. This fine monument in coral pink stone, was built at the end of the 13th century and is worth a visit.

You next go down to the village of Boroneddu and head for Ghilarza, a fair-sized town with a wide range of services available.

Continue now towards nearby Abbasanta. A few miles from Abbasanta there are signs indicating the gigantic Nuraghe Losa. This is one of the most important traces of the civilization that developed in Sardinia between the 15th and the 6th centuries B.C. Around the original 3-storey conical tower, perhaps used as a place of worship, stand fortified towers and curtain walls, which made this complex a real defensive stronghold.

Back in Abbasanta, take the secondary road that passes through the wooded countryside of Sant'Agostino to Santulussurgiu. The town appears suddenly, lying in a deep hollow sheltered from the wind. Santulussurgiu has an old tradition of sheep-rearing and horse-riding. This is an excellent place to stop for lunch; try the local dairy products and superb brandy.

Leaving Santulussurgiu, head for San Leonardo—the junction is 2.5 miles (4 kilometers) from town—through stupendous scenery of woods and mountain pastures. In this town, you might want to stop at the springs known as "Siete Fuentes" and see the fine Romanesque church.

From here, return to the crossroads and follow the indications for Cuglieri, again traveling through beautiful countryside. From the Passo della Madonnina you will see the wide view of the sea to the west of Sardinia and, eventually, come into the city.

Cuglieri is the old capital of the region and boasts many modern services, including hotels, restaurants and craft shops. After visiting the city, continue your excursion, passing through Scano, Sagama, Tinnura, Flussio and Magomadas, which are important craft centers. When you reach the village of Tresnuraghes, continue along via Cuglieri to Santa Caterina di Pittinurri, Riola Sardo and Nurachi, on the SS 292, between low hills and the dunes of the Sinis. From here it is only a short distance to Oristano.

THE EASTERN ROUTE

Arbatax, the little town overlooking the sea at the tip of the short peninsula of Capo Bellavista, has become a popular resort in recent years.

The gastronomical tradition is excellent, making use of the basic ingredients supplied by the fishing boats from the harbor.

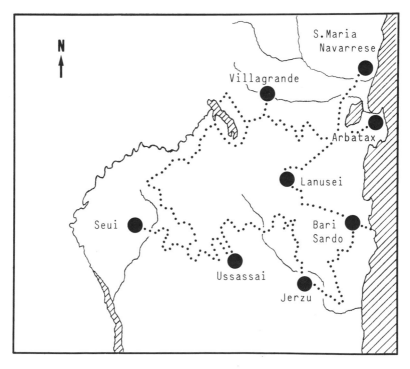

Sardinia's Eastern Route

From Arbatax, the eastern route extends to Tortoli, then heads northwards on the SS 125. After passing through the villages of Girasole and Lotzorai, turn right for Santa Maria Navarrese. This is a renowned seaside resort with a fine beach overlooked by a 17th century watch-tower. You might want to visit the 11th century church here before returning to Tortoli to continue the excursion along SS 198. Follow the road for 1.8 miles (3 kilometers), until the first crossroads on the right. Take the side road to Villagrande Strisaili. Prior to reaching the town, the road climbs with a series of bends and the views over the sea become gradually wider, framed by rugged mountain peaks.

Villagrande Strisaili is a large village with old traditions of sheep and cattle rearing. An attractive place surrounded by cool woods, Villagrande produces excellent cheeses and famous ham products.

Leaving Villagrande, proceed amid mountain pastures and oak woods for 2.5 miles (4 kilometers) and join the SS 389. After another 1.2 miles (2 kilometers) you will come to the little village of Villanova Strisaili on the banks of the artificial lake of the Upper Flumendosa. The waters of the lake, the rich vegetation and the fine air give the place an almost alpine flavor.

From Villanova Strisaili, go back up the SS 389 for 3 miles (5 kilometers) to the railway station at Villagrande where you turn right at the crossroads and take the secondary road for Arqueri.

This is a rather tiring stretch, but the route allows you to discover one of the most extraordinary natural environments in Sardinia, the likes of which would be difficult to find even outside the island. After flanking the south slope of the mountain basin of the Flumendosa, the road winds along the mountainside between the tormented canyon of the river on the right and the unspoiled, wild and mighty peaks of Cuccuru Mufloni and Monte Tonneri to the left. Here is also the Perda Liana (Flat Stone), a compact rock formation of enormous size with a completely flat top.

In this haven for large and small game, you may see tens of thousands of woodpigeons flying over the valley in mile-long flocks from October to March. It is not rare to also encounter boar and mouflons, though you have to seek them out. When you get to Cantoniera Arqueri, join the SS 198, turn right and after 6 miles (9 kilometers) you will come to Seui.

Seui has an economy based on farming, sheep rearing and vineyard cultivation; and it produces a famous wine. The village stands in a typical position, for the area, with all the streets running up and downhill.

From here, go back up the SS 198, carrying on past the crossroads at Cantoniera Arqueri towards the village of Ussassai. The road now winds through rocky scenery to the crossroads for Ierzu. Turn right and pass through the villages of Osini and Ulassai, overhung by dizzy rocky peaks.

Close to Ulassai are the stupendous caves of "Su Marmuri". A visit to them will take at least 3 hours.

Now the road runs along the west face of the deep valley of the river Pardu, offering the apocalyptic vision of the east face on which stand the ruins of the village of Gairo Vecchia; destroyed by landslides, the village had to be rebuilt on firmer ground. Shortly, you will come to Jerzu.

The hard work of the inhabitants of Jerzu has transformed the countryside. Here you'll find gentle vineyards extending across the land. From these vineyards come the grapes, which make Jerzu the capital of "Canonau" wine, most of which is exported.

Continuing your journey, you come to the crossroads with the SS 125 (to eastern Sardinia). Turn left and descend quickly towards the bottom of the valley, in a pleasant countryside of terraced vineyards, interrupted here and there by patches of woods. A straight road leads to Bari Sardo.

In recent years this little village has been considerably developed for tourist and residential purposes. The beach at Torre di Bari, just 3 miles (5 kilometers) away, is quite pleasant with its fine sand and shady woods.

Going back via Bari Sardo, take the SS 390 which, after Loceri winds up through evocative scenery: on the right is the wide open sea, and on the left the harsh rocky peaks of the mountain range. This will take you to Lanusei.

164

The chief town of the Ogliastra region, Lanusei is a bright, attractive place, with fine buildings, tidy squares, and plenty of services and accommodations. This is a very well-known holiday center during the summer months. Walks in the hills and pleasant parks complete the local attractions.

From Lanusei, take the SS 198 which goes down towards the sea after passing through the tiny village of Ilbono. The countryside gradually becomes farmland as you descend to the plain of the river Corongiu. You'll return through Tortoli to Arbatax, where your excursion began.

THE NORTHERN ROUTE

The northern route begins in St. Teresa di Gallura, a lively town at the extreme north of the island, situated in a panoramic position dominating the Bonifacio Straits. This town managed to transform its modest economy based on fishing and agriculture over a short period of time into a flourishing tourist industry with the participation of practically the entire working population. Aside from its attraction as a seaside resort, St. Teresa offers splendid landscapes with rugged coastlines and sheer cliffs, promontories and granite rocks shaped by the wind into thousands of incredible forms.

From St. Teresa take the road towards Capo Testa through a fantastic landscape of multicolored granite rock formations. Crossing the Due Mari isthmus you reach the promontory of Capo Testa projecting towards the open sea. Along the edges of the cliffs one can still see traces of Roman excavations that provided the granite for the dockside at Ostia, the ancient port of Rome. The stone blocks were transported there by sea.

Returning to St. Teresa, take the SS 200 as far as the crossroad for Aglientu, some 18.6 miles (30 kilometers) from St. Teresa, along a road that crosses similar landscape to that which you have left, with rugged rocks, small woods of oak trees and thick Mediterranean bush. The journey continues through an apocalyptic environment as far as Aggius.

Among cyclopean granite rocks shaped like steeples and pinnacles lies Aggius, which is similarly built of granite, as

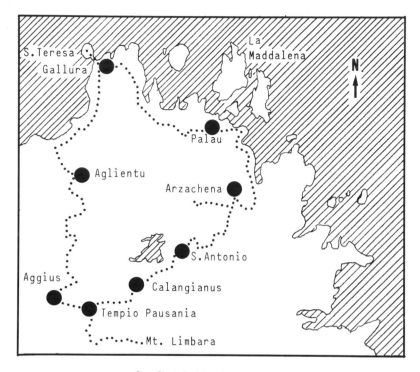

Sardinia's Northern Route

though to camouflage itself in the landscape. The visitor is sure to find a warm welcome here. The town is the home of one of the oldest styles of Sardinian folk song: the singing is Gregorian-like, based on a soprano soloist, with the second and third voices, and the basses, acting as harmonic background—all of which gives the effect of an organ. A fine sparkling wine is made from the local grapes.

From Aggius the route continues to Tempio Pausania, an ancient town which preserves a certain nobility in its severe architectural style. The fine squares are meeting places for the lively and enthusiastic population. Among the attractions, Tempio offers an interesting carnival with dances, festivities and the consumption of traditional cakes.

Leaving Tempio, take the road towards Monte Limbara, a panoramic route that rises up a series of winding bends. The landscape is decidedly mountainous, with thick woodland, where the newly planted conifers mix with oaks and Mediterranean bush. Here again, the granite rocks form strange and eerie shapes as a result of centuries of wind. The road winds upward for 10.6 miles (17 kilometers) as far as the Villicciola of Our Lady of the Snow, to within a few hundred yards of the Balestrieri peak.

Returning to Tempio, follow the road to Calangianus, a principal city for cork manufacturing. A range of ornamental and useful products made from cork are on sale. The cards and postcards printed on thin leaves of cork are particularly attractive.

From Calangianus take the SS 427 toward Sant'Antonio. Take the turn-off for Luogosanto. The asphalt gives way to a country track after 2.8 miles (4.5 kilometers). Another mile down the track takes you to the sacred location of Li Muri. It is a collective megalithic burial ground also known as "the giants' tomb." This dates back to the 3rd millenium B.C., the period of the cult dedicated to the Mediterranean Mother Goddess. This was a religion common to all the peoples of the Southern Mediterranean.

The tomb is designed to house a number of corpses and has a narrow corridor 43 feet long by 3 feet wide (13 meters long by 1 meter wide), with walls built of rock slabs that were originally covered with other slabs. The corpses were set in a crouching, almost fetal position. Around the tomb a great number stones were placed. The burial place at Li Muri, like many prehistoric sacred sites, is pervaded by a sense of mystery and magic.

After visiting Li Muri, return to the crossroads and continue on to Arzachena. This large town has had a boost from the tourist industry. Bars, restaurants, shops and boutiques welcome the visitor. Notice the curious rocks shaped by the wind to take on the form of "mushrooms" and "tortoises."

From Arzachena take the road to Cannigione, Laconia, and Isuledda, along the beautiful coastline of the Arzzachena Gulf, to reach Capo d'Orso, some 4.3 miles (7 kilometers) past Cannigione.

Capo d'Orso got its name from the rock formation that appears to be a gigantic polar bear dominating the sea. As you look out over the gulf from Liscia di Vacca to Punta Falcone, the scenic prospect is one not readily found in other parts of the Mediterranean.

From here, the road goes down to Palau, the point of embarcation for the tiny island of La Maddalena. The charm of the town and cordiality of the people make La Maddalena well worth visiting.

The route continues along SS 133, and then the SS 133B, through thick woods and rock formations, with occasional views of the sea, until you arrive once again at St. Teresa di Gallura.

The Sicilian Excursion

If you're a lover of history, archaeology, nature and/or fine cuisine, you are in for a love affair with Sicily. The lure of this island, the largest in the Mediterranean Sea, is hard to resist.

The Sicily route covers a distance of 177 miles (285 kilome-

The unique rock formations of Sardinia.

ters) and offers some of the finest attractions in Agrigento, Enna, Piazza Armerina, Catania and Syracuse. Traveling this itinerary with a bicycle takes from 7 to 10 days, depending on how much time you spend admiring local sites. All the roads you will be traveling are in good condition.

The people of Sicily are a combination of ancient races. Their rich past has seen the crossing of Phoenicians, Greeks, Carthaginians, Romans, Byzantines, Saracens and Normans. During the past 300 years, Germans, French and Spanish have also invaded and left their imprint on the population and its traditions.

When the Greeks first colonized Sicily, their new home was called Akragas. When the Romans and Carthaginians plagued the territory in 210 B.C., the city became Agrigentum. One of the high points of a visit to this ancient town is the Valley of the Temples. This is a series of 20 Greek structures, of which the best preserved is the Temple of Concordia. Most tourists also find the Doric Temple of Hercules of interest. It is believed to be one of the oldest, dating to the 6th century B.C. The Temple of Hera Licinia boasts 25 of its original columns while the Olympian Zeus Temple is the largest of the Hellenistic antiquities, with a base of 370 by 184.4 feet (113 by 56.6 meters).

Of the remaining 16 ruins, special effort should be made to see the Temple of Castor, Pollux, Vulcan and Aesculapius. Also in the vicinity visitors will find the Sanctuary of Demeter from the 7th century B.C., the Tomb of Theron and the Oratory of Phalaris.

Each of these sites has special points of interest for archaeology enthusiasts as well as those who just come along for the feel of ancient Greek and Roman life. The ruins can usually be seen between the hours of 9 a.m. and one hour before sunset. There is also a museum of archaeology at Agrigento exhibiting a fine collection of artifacts found within the ruins.

From Agrigento, the itinerary takes a north-eastern direction along Highway 122 for 57 miles (92 kilometers), passing through Caltanissetta, and eventually taking you to Enna.

Enna is a name unfamiliar to many. Yet from here you have one of the finest panoramas in all of Sicily. Located in the

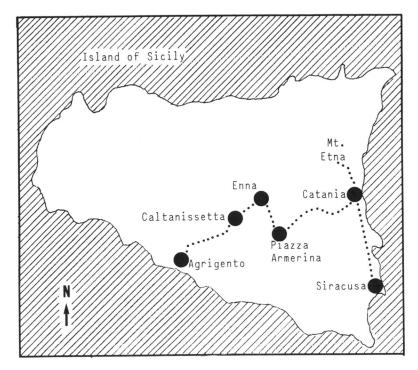

The Sicily Route

center of the island, Enna boasts the Castle of Lombardia which is open to the public during the daylight hours and a breathtaking view—the best being from the Pisan Tower.

Not far from Enna, heading south on Highway 117 (bis), is the hill town of Piazza Armerina. While the town itself does not offer much for the visitor, the famous excavations of Casale and the Imperial Villa, just a short distance away on the road to Mazarino, do.

According to archaeologists, the villa was constructed between the 3rd and 4th centuries A.D. The 5 Roman mosaics which decorate the walls are considered the best preserved of their period. Some of the more exotic scenes depicted in the tesserae art work are the maidens in bikinis, the bathers, sea

---

Old city near Francavilla, Sicily.

Selinunte ruins near Catania, along the Sicilian route.

myths, a massage parlor, hunting, beasts of prey and the Labors of Hercules. The villa is thought to have been built by Maximianus Herculeus, co-emperor with Diocletian.

From Piazza Armerina head east on Highway 288 to Catania, a distance of about 40 miles (65 kilometers). Many see Catania as a typical Sicilian city. Actually, it is that and more. Piazza del Duomo, surrounded by its elegant 18th century buildings and Elephant Fountains, gives you a feel for the town. But it is the cathedral—built in 1693 by Vaccarini—with its masterful facade and fine interior art that interests most tourists.

Not far away is the Ursino Castle which was constructed under Frederick II. Its 4 round corner towers, fosses, 16th century windows and great inner halls make this an attraction for both young and old. Catania also contains the ruins of a Greek theater and Roman amphitheater, the latter dating from the 2nd century A.D.

From Catania, head north following the signs to Mount Etna. This is an 18.6 mile/30-kilometer excursion. In Greek mythology, Zeus crushed the multi-headed, viper-riddled dragon, Typhoeus, under Etna. It was also here that Hephaestus, the god of fire and blacksmithing, made his home, aided by the one-eyed Cyclops. A trip up Etna is both interesting and exciting. Since it is a live volcano, you never know what to expect. (See Part IX, "Hot Foot Adventures," for more information on exploring Mount Etna.)

After you have visited Etna, return to Catania and head south along the coastal road #114, for 36 miles (58 kilometers) until you come to the city of Syracuse.

According to Cicero, Syracuse was the finest and largest of all Greek cities. Legends have surrounded this sea-bordered region ever since the Corinthian Greeks settled in 414 B.C. Treacherous battles between these peoples and the Greeks of Athens took place here. In fact, over 7,000 Athenean prisoners were taken and closed up in stone quarters—which can still be seen—to die of thirst and malnutrition. Aeschylus came here to write his tragedies and here Epicarmus brought his comedies to be performed in the Greek Theater.

Today, Syracuse is a booming industrial town, but just outside the city limits you'll find the ruins of the theaters, Palazzolo Acreide with its Temple of Aphrodite, and the Roman Amphitheater. Here also are the Altar of Hieron which was built in the latter part of the 3rd century B.C. for public sacrifices and the noteworthy group of stone quarries that were used for death pits. The archaeological sites of Syracuse are open to the public from 9 a.m. to 1 p.m. and from 4 to 8 p.m.

The more modern section of Syracuse also offers an outstanding array of Christian catacombs and basilicas which display the art and architecture of the city's Byzantine, Gothic and Renaissance periods. The catacombs of St. John draw many visitors. These honeycombed tunnels once housed the dead, and acted as hiding places during the time of Christian persecution. The entrance to the catacombs can be found at the end of Viale San Giovanni, just down the road from the church of the same name.

Tuscany on Two Wheels

Encompassing the splendor of Florence and its renowned Hill Towns, Tuscany is undoubtedly one of Italy's most picturesque regions. For centuries visitors have been drawn to the area, taking in its Renaissance art, rolling countryside and warm hospitality. Today, through La Roncola, an agency working in collaboration with the local tourist office, one can see the wonders of Tuscany on two wheels.

La Roncola bicycle excursions take you along slow and relaxing rides, exploring old roads and villages as well as visiting farms and vineyards. Among its one-day excursions are tours of Chianti, of Giaggiolo, and of the Pesa Valley. The Chianti tour leaves Florence every Tuesday from July through September. The others operate on various days through July and August.

Other bicycle outings offered by La Roncola include: a 3-day Sienese tour, which takes in San Gimignano, Siena, Castellina

Tuscan olive groves.

and back to Florence; and a tour of Mugello, another 3-day venture.

For those who are really adventurous, there is also a 10-day tour of Tuscany called "La Toscana in Bicicletta." This excursion includes Florence, the Hill Towns and seaside areas of the region. This trip is only offered twice during the year—in July and August.

All of La Roncola's bicycle adventures in Tuscany include an experienced guide (English and Italian speaking), 10-speed touring bicycles (Bianchi), meals, a visit to a vineyard for wine tasting and, for longer trips, accommodations. Cost for the one-day tours runs from 76,000 to 89,000 lire depending on the number of participants. Three-day excursions range from 229,000 to 278,000 lire. The ten-day outing is 880,000 lire. Anyone participating with his or her own bicycle will receive a discount to 50,000 lire.

For more information on bicycling through Tuscany, write La Roncola (address in Appendix A).

The Tuscan countryside.

Mountain Biking

In recent years mountain biking, which began in the United States, has become popular among a select group of bicyclers in Italy. As a result, the Mountain Biking Club of Italy was organized to provide information and assistance to those partaking in the sport.

Mountain biking utilizes all-terrain bikes, designed for off-road use. In Italy, such bikes are used to travel dry river beds, wooded trails, and country paths. Some adventurous bikers have even ventured down shallow streams on these vehicles.

With the cooperation of its members, the Mountain Biking Club of Italy has prepared itineraries where you can enjoy off-road biking throughout the country. If you are interested in this sport, address questions and information requests to the General Secretary, Mountain Biking Club of Italy, Via Durini 24, 20133 Milan, Italy.

PART VI

RIVER TRIPS

Italy, with more than 5,280 miles (8,397 kilometers) of coast-line, 1,500 freshwater lakes and thousands of rivers, is an excellent place for canoeing adventures. Over the past decade canoeing has become extremely popular in Italy, and there are currently about 60 canoe clubs throughout the peninsula (see Appendix F for a complete listing).

Generally, rivers in Italy are short; the longest, the Po, is only 400 miles (644 kilometers). Three of the country's major rivers flow into the Ionian Sea, while two flow into the Adriatic after crossing the Puglia region. Several rivers begin in the Apennine mountain range, flowing through the regions of Molise, Abruzzi and Marche. The Volturno River in Campania, the Tiber from Rome, and the Arno, which runs through Florence and Pisa, are the major rivers flowing into the Tyrrhenian Sea. Liguria, the province which encompasses the north-western coast, contains several short, swift rivers. The true pride of the Italians, however, is the Po.

Beginning in the Monviso district, the Po crosses the Plain of Lombardy, traverses Turin and Cremona, and eventually empties into a large delta south of Venice. Numerous tributaries empty into the Po, particularly along its left bank. The second largest river in Italy is the Adige, which runs for 254 miles (409 kilometers) through such centers as Verona and Adria, near Venice.

Italy offers superb rivers for canoeing.

While Italy's major rivers can be interesting to travel, particularly if one enjoys passing through historical cities, most canoeists prefer the smaller, lesser-known waterways. Many of these offer spectacular natural settings and, in some cases, rapids.

The major problem of most visitors to Italy is locating and obtaining the needed equipment. Overcoming this obstacle is not as difficult as it may seem. As previously mentioned, there are nearly 60 canoe clubs throughout the country. Most of these offer rental equipment, maps, advice and even organized outings with guides. Another option is the many sporting goods outlets which specialize in canoeing equipment. Most often these are located near rivers or freshwater lakes and offer daily rentals. If you'd like to experience open-sea canoeing, this can normally be done through one of the many boat rental operations found along the coasts.

Another choice would be to contact an outfitter who specializes in organizing river adventures. One such outfitter is Club-avventour (address in Appendix A). Located in Rome, Club-avventour, is affiliated with the Italian Federation of River Canoeing. It not only organizes group and individual outings, but offers such services as canoe and accessory rentals, maps for canoers, and information on camping grounds along various river routes. Even if you are not interested in joining an organized trip, it would be worthwhile to write this organization for their free information.

Canadian style canoes are rarely seen in Italy, though many do exist. More likely you will find various types of kayaks.

For The Beginner

If you have never canoed, but would like to give it a try, Italy offers an excellent opportunity to do so at the School of Canoeing, held each summer in the Alpine region of the Aosta Valley. There are two schools, conducted by expert canoeists Maurizio and Emanuele Bernasconi. The first is in the village of Courmayeur, the second in Varallo.

The courses take you from the beginner stage through the various levels of canoeing with daily lessons over a week-long period. Also available is a rafting adventure down one of the local swift-water rivers.

For more information write Maurizio Bernasconi, Via Lomellina 46, 20133 Milan, Italy.

Rafting Adventures

In addition to the School of Canoeing's rafting program, you can also shoot the rapids of the Alpine rivers along the French-Italian border with Wildwater-Expeditions S.A., situated 15 minutes from Mont Blanc. This outfitter provides thrilling 4- to 6-hour rafting adventures, complete with gear, transportation and friendly companions. Excursions take place from June to October for adventurers 14 years old and up.

Wildwater-Expeditions' rafting tours are not for those who enjoy sitting back and watching the world go by. Participants are issued paddles and expected to do their part to control the raft as it races down Alpine white waters.

Prices and details of each expedition are available from Wildwater-Expeditions, Il Punto, Centro Sportivo Communale, Rue Saint Marc 3, 11017 Morgex (Aoste), Italy.

Canoeing Routes

There are thousands of good canoeing routes in Italy—far too many to list in a single book, let alone a chapter. The following itineraries, however, will save you time and provide enjoyable canoeing.

Each listing includes a point of embarkation, debarkation, a brief description of the river and route, and where to obtain assistance and/or rental equipment.

ALCANTARA RIVER (Sicily)

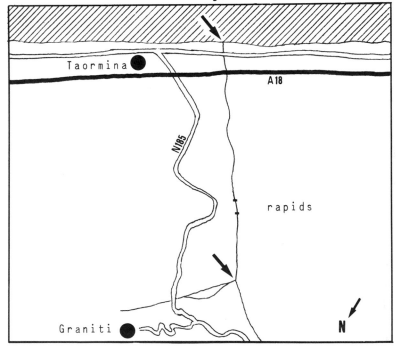

Embarkation: Graniti
Debarkation: The Ionion Sea
Length: 6 miles (9 kilometers)

Route: Beginning at the bridge in Graniti, travel southeast for 6 miles (9 kilometers) to the Ionian Sea. One of the highlights is a short rapids half-way through the route.

Assistance: Kayac Club Zingaro, Palermo or Canottieri Siracusa Sez. Canoa.

ARAXISI (Sardinia)

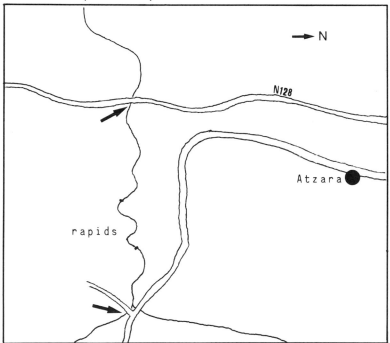

Embarkation: Bridge between Atzara and Aritzo
Debarkation: Bridge on the SS 128 highway
Length: 3.7 miles (6 kilometers)

Route: From the bridge between Atzara and Aritzo, head west. The river quickly forks. Turn left. After a few curves, you'll encounter a series of rapids. Following the rapids, there is a mile of so of easy paddling before debarking at the SS 128 bridge. At certain times of the year, floating vegetation can make the route slightly more dangerous.

Assistance: Canoa Club Cagliari.

BORBERA RIVER (Piedmont)

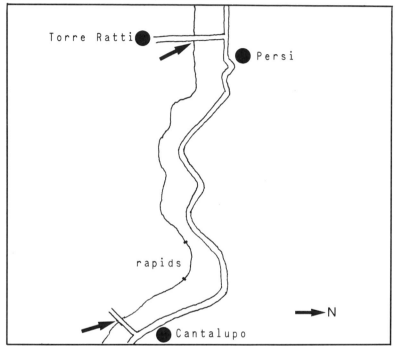

Embarkation: Cantalupo
Debarkation: Persi (right bank)
Length: 5.2 miles (8.5 kilometers)

Route: Enter the river at Cantalupo, heading west. About 2 miles (3.2 kilometers) along the route you will encounter a section of rapids. After 5.2 miles (8.5 kilometers) debark at Persi, along the right bank.

Assistance: Canoa Club Alessandria.

TANARO RIVER (Piedmont)

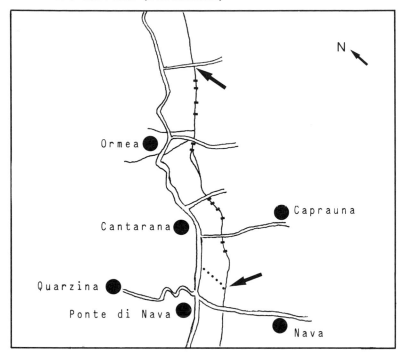

Embarkation: Bridge at Nava
Debarkation: Cartiera di Ormea (left bank)
Length: 5 miles (8 kilometers)

Route: This route is not advised for beginners or those who are not experienced in swift-water canoeing. Along the route you will encounter narrow passages and a number of rapids.

Assistance: Canoe Club Cuneo.

TICINO RIVER (Lombardy)

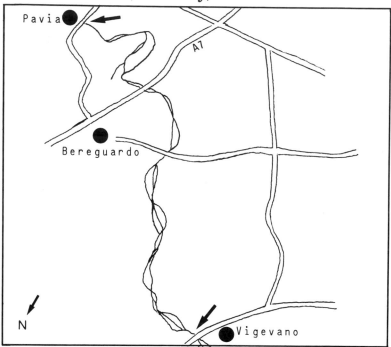

Embarkation: Vigevano
Debarkation: Pavia
Length: 25 miles (40 kilometers)

Route: Entering the water from the iron bridge at Vigevano, head south along this relatively easy river route.

Assistance: C.U.S. Pavia, Canotteri Ticino, Canoe Club Vigevano.

RIVER NOCE (Trentino-Alto Adige)

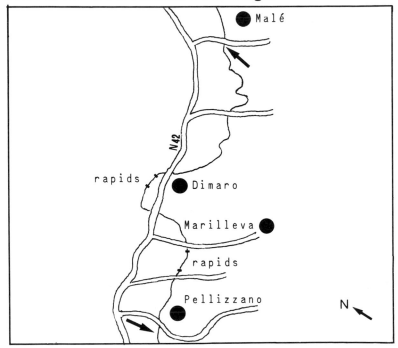

Embarkation: Pellizzano
Debarkation: Malè
Length: 10 miles (16 kilometers)

Route: Embark just before the bridge in Pallizzano, head north-east past curves, tiny rapids and picturesque villages before debarking in the city of Malè.

Assistance: Canoa Club Trento.

RIENZA RIVER (Trentino-Alto Adige)

Embarkation: S. Lorenzo
Debarkation: Rio di Pusteria
Length: 11 miles (18 kilometers)

Route: This is a beautiful route beginning at the bridge of San Lorenzo and ending 11 miles (18 kilometers) downstream in the village of Rio di Pusteria. Debark before entering Lake Rio di Pusteria. This is a large river with easy canoeing.

Assistance: Canoe Club Bressanone.

NATISONE (Friuli-Venezia Giulia)

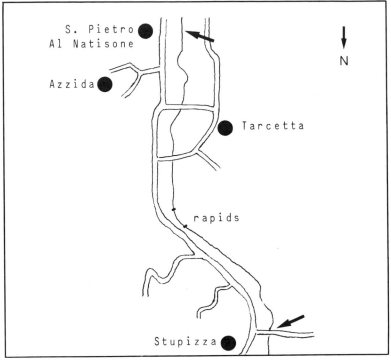

Embarkation: Stupizza
Debarkation: San Pietro al Natisone
Length: 7.5 miles (12 kilometers)

Route: The Natisone river runs through valleys and mountains from the embarkation point—the bridge in Stupizza—to the debarkation in San Pietro al Natison. Along the 7.5-mile/12-kilometer route is one section of rapids, about 3 miles (4.8 kilometers) into the trip.

Assistance: Canoa Club Udine, Canoa Club Natisone.

BURANO RIVER (Marche)

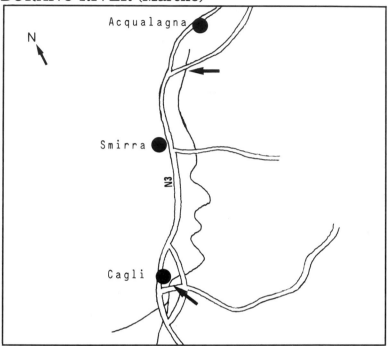

Embarkation: Cagli
Debarkation: Acqualagna
Length: 7.5 miles (12 kilometers)

Route: Entering the Burano from the left bank at Cagli, head north-east along a winding but easy route. During certain times of the year, floating vegetation may gather at bends in the river. Debark at the bridge in Acqualagna.

Assistance: Canoa Club Valmetauro

RIVER SANGRO (Abruzzi)

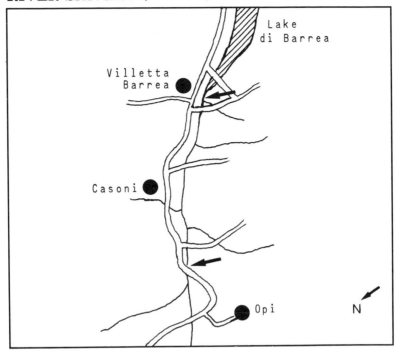

Embarkation: Opi
Debarkation: Lake Barrea
Length: 5 miles (8 kilometers)

Route: Just outside the mountain village of Opi, enter the Sangro and head west. At points the river is fast-flowing and a number of mountain streams filter into it along the 5-mile/8-kilometer route. Eventually, the river expands into Lake Barrea, where you can debark, or explore further downstream.

Assistance: No local assistance; the nearest organization for equipment is the Gruppo Canoa Roma.

LAO RIVER (Calabria)

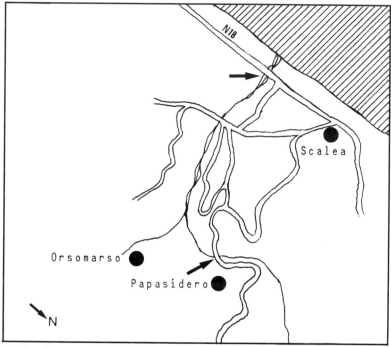

Embarkation: Papasidero
Debarkation: Tyrrhenian Sea
Length: 11 miles (18 kilometers)

Route: From the bridge in the town of Papasidero, ride the downstream currents along the 11-mile/18-kilometer route leading to the open sea. Halfway along the route you will have to leave the river to get around a blockade.

Assistance: The nearest canoe organization is Canoa Club Policastro. However, you may be able to rent canoes in the coastal villages of Scalea or Diamante.

PART VII

CLIMBING ADVENTURES

Spurred by the achievements of renowned alpinist Reinhold Messner and the country's extensive mountainous regions, Italians have fallen in love with climbing. Numerous schools and clubs dedicated to traditional mountaineering and free climbing have emerged throughout the peninsula over the past decade.

Wherever your personal climbing interests lie, you are sure to find a challenge in Italy. Not only are there exciting climbs in the northern Alps, but throughout the Apennines, along much of the country's coast and on most of the islands.

Many mountaineers are attracted to Italy's famous peaks. Heading the list is the Mont Blanc massif, which extends skyward for 15,771 feet (4,807 meters) to surpass the 15,203-foot/ 4,634-meter Monte Rosa, as well as the 14,688 feet (4,477 meters) of the Matterhorn, the 10,964 feet (3,342 meters) of the Marmolada in the Dolomites, and the 10,336 feet (3,150 meters) of the Cima Brenta. In the Apennines, the Gran Sasso offers the highest adventure at 9,560 feet (2,914 meters).

In the southern regions good climbing can be found along the western coast from Gaeta to Terracina and the southern shores from Salerno to Reggio Calabria. The Sila Mountain range in the National Park of Calabria provides some fine

Climbing is one of the most popular sports in Italy.

sites for free climbing, while the islands of Capri and Sardinia are very popular among climbers for their natural rock formations.

Some tourist offices—particularly those in the northern regions—can provide you with information on where to climb (see Appendix C for a listing of tourist offices and addresses). A few will even send you a free booklet on local climbs, which includes photos of rock formations and the better-known approaches.

It goes without saying that all climbing sports require preparation and equipment. In Italy, it especially calls for pre-planning. Before any climb you should gather information on the rock formations and known approaches. These may be obtained from any local Italian Alpine Club (CAI) office (see Appendix D for a listing of addresses). If you are planning a major climb that will take several days, you should also register your route and time schedule with the nearest CAI office. They will then keep track of your progress and be prepared to intervene with the Mountain Rescue Organization in the event of an emergency.

The Mountain Rescue Organization (CSA), a division of the CAI, has offices throughout the country. Its stations are well equipped and members of the group are trained to help mountaineers both on rock and on glaciers. Dogs to find people under avalanches and helicopters are also available through the CSA.

Another sub-division of the Italian Alpine Club which many foreign climbers find helpful is the Society of Guides. The organization is at the disposal of mountaineers for every type of ascent. Guides are easily available in every area; you need only apply at the nearest ACI office, tourist office, or with the guides themselves.

Arco: Italy's free climbing capital

Of all the locations where mountaineering is practiced, the tiny center of Arco, situated among the pre-Alps of north-central Italy, has emerged as the country's climbing capital. Here traditional mountain climbing and free climbing are both available. Because of this, Arco hosts a number of annual climbing competitions and mountaineering schools.

There are more than 250 noted rock climbing sites in the vicinity of Arco, including the famed "Via di Roccia" and the "Grotte del'Alto Garda." Fifty-five of these locations have been designated free climbing routes, while the others are suggested for traditional mountain climbers.

The area also offers excellent hiking and watersports in nearby Lake Garda, the largest fresh-water lake in Italy.

From April to September, week-long schools are conducted in Arco for climbers of all levels. Past schools included at least one instructor who spoke English, French and German. Costs of the schools, which include camping accommodations, vary according to the level of difficulty. For more information on Arco's climbing schools, write Coral Climb, Via della Resistenza 7, 25014 Castenedolo (Bs), Italy or Centro di Arrampicata, c/o Camping "Arco" Località Prabi, 38062 Arco (Trento) Italy.

If you plan to climb in Arco, it is advisable to contact the latter group for information on local rock formations and, if desired, a guide. You can also contact the local tourist office for assistance: Azienda Autonoma di Cura e Soggiorno, Viale delle Palme 1, 38062 Arco, Italy.

On Mont Blanc.

Mont Blanc Adventures

While Arco holds the crown for free climbing excitement, Mont Blanc is without a doubt supreme for high-altitude climbing thrills. Much of the year the slopes of Mont Blanc are snow-covered. During the summer, many of the slopes lose their winter appearance and become high-rising rock masses.

For experienced mountaineers, excursions on Mont Blanc are both thrilling and easy—if planned correctly. There are several refuges on the mountain where food and shelter can be obtained. In fact, it is a good idea to plan your route in such a way as to take in a number of refuges.

There is an excellent school for mountaineering on Mont Blanc run by Courmayeur's Society of Guides. This organization can also provide general information on current mountain conditions, approaches, equipment, assistance and guides. Those planning to take on Mont Blanc should contact the group at: Società delle Guide di Courmayeur, C.P. 45, 11013 Courmayeur (AO) Italy.

PART VIII

SPELUNKING ADVENTURES

Why people go into dark, unknown tunnels and caves below the earth's surface is a mystery to some. Yet, for many, the urge to know what secrets lie within the subterranean darkness compel them to enter, explore, and venture ever deeper.

Anthropologist Carleton S. Coon stated that to explore a cave gives an ordinary man enough of a feeling of power to make up for the fact that he will never be President of the United States nor Pope at Rome, and enough responsibility and opportunity for decision-making to satisfy the Odysseus and Solomon lurking in all of us.

Italy is a perfect place to begin such an odyssey. With nearly 21,000 noted caves and an estimated 2–3,000 yet to be explored, Italy is one of Europe's leading countries for underground adventures.

Since prehistoric times man has utilized caves, first for habitat, then military shelters, and finally for storage purposes. In Italy, caves were inhabited off-and-on by families and bands of hunters until the time when agriculture came onto the scene 7–8,000 years ago. When cave dwelling faded, the ex-inhabitants left behind traces of their ancient lifestyles buried among layers of soil and painted on the cavern walls. Such

4.502	Friuli V. Giulia	646	Piemonte
2.576	Veneto	631	Emilia Romagna
2.500	Lombardia	500	Marche
1.620	Sardegna	500	Trentino A. Adige
1.600	Puglia	450	Sicilia
1.207	Liguria	250	Calabria
967	Lazio	181 {	Abruzzi / Molise
947	Campania		
756	Toscana	160	Basilicata
727	Umbria	24	Valle d'Aosta

Number of known caves in Italy, by region.

remains have been found in many Italian caves, including the extensive Grotta del Vento in the region of Tuscany. This particular cave begins in Fornovolasco, a town in the Apuan Alps between Massa and Lucca.

One of the finest examples of Palaeolithic graffiti of bulls and oxen is located near Papadidero, on the road from Scalea to Mormanno, in southern Calabria. In 1961, this cavern, now known as the shelter of "Il Romito," was discovered and its cave drawings of 10,000 B.C. brought to light.

There are 3 basic types of caves and Italy has fine examples of each. Karstenite caves, formed by water flowing through limestone, are perhaps the most picturesque of all underground dens, with their stalactites (which hang from the ceiling) and stalagmites (which stick up from the floor).

Seaside grottoes, though similar in that they are formed by water currents, are more like huge holes in the side of the land base rather than the extended tunnel form of the karstenites. The seaside versions often have a small entrance and open into large, hollowed-out spaces, as with the Blue Grotto of Capri.

The third type is the animal-dug cave. Little is known about how these came about, yet they were used by early man, who often extended them for his own comfort. In more recent times, man began digging his own caves, often in the form of catacombs. These can be found in cities throughout the peninsula.

Seaside grottos are abundant in Italy.

Characteristics of Italian Caves

As a rule, karstenite caves in Italy have high humidity, which causes the beautiful stalagmite and stalactite formations. Humidity runs from 75 to 100% almost all year, with the exception of the summer months when it drops a little due to the lack of surface rainfall.

Temperatures in some Italian caves, such as the Grotte di Castellana, remain constant throughout the year with an average of 50 °F (15 °C).

As with most caves, those found in Italy have their share of subterranean life. Nesting owls can be found in some winding passages and chambers, and many harmless bats live in dark ceiling nooks. Rare types of rodents also exists in the flooring of many caves and may be heard occasionally fleeing for cover when explorers pass by. Scientists have also found rare species of blind grasshoppers, millipedes, crustaceans, and earthworms in undisturbed dark areas.

Of the natural, karstenite caves in Italy, about 30 have been adapted for tourists with lights, guides and, in some locations, boats that carry you on an underground lake through the vast caverns. Some of the more noted caves of this type include the Grotta della Basura in Toirano (Liguria) which is rich in natural beauty and contains traces of ancient inhabitants; the Grotta Gigante, in the region of Friuli-Venezia, with an enormous chamber the size of St. Peter's Basilica in Rome; the Grotta Genga, located between Iesi and Fabriano in the region of Marche; the Grotta del Bue Marino, on the island of Sardinia; and in Apulia, the Grotte di Castellana.

To get a feel for spelunking, tourist caves are excellent and safe. What fascinates most adventurers, however, are the thousands of small or unexplored caves that promise true mystery and excitement. A good region to begin your search is in Venezia Giulia, where some 4,502 caves are known to exist. In Veneto, 2,576 caves have been mapped, in Lombardy 2,500, in Sardinia 1,620, in Puglia 1,600, in Liguria 1,207, and the regions of Lazio and Campania contain nearly 1,000 caves each. Other regions boast between 760 and 24 noted caves. The one area that is not recommended for spelunking is Sicily.

Subterranean Safety

Exploring a cave can be an unforgettable experience if done correctly. This includes proper equipment, training, and physical preparation. Even caves of moderate depths and dimensions pose serious dangers if not approached with care. In some cases, even minor mistakes can be disastrous. Once underground, there are few means of alerting rescue groups if an accident happens. For this reason, you should never explore alone. Even when exploring with a partner some person or group, such as the local Club Alpino Italiano (CAI), should be alerted to the fact that you plan to enter a certain cave at a given time and told when you will return. Then, upon completion of your venture, advise them that you have returned safe and sound.

Spelunking is a tiring sport, particularly where greater depths are to be explored. You should be in good physical shape for such adventuring. A good rule of thumb is to take plenty of time and rest when needed. Rushing and fatigue are two major causes of accidents.

Never enter a cave without the proper equipment and training (some of the organizations below can assist with the latter). A good hard-hat with lamp incorporated is essential. Without this, moving and exploring in subterranean environments is impossible. Most experienced spelunkers prefer helmets which have a double illumination system: gas with battery-powered reserve.

The presence of water and the low temperatures means you will need special clothing such as a bib-type waterproof suit, jacket, and boots. Also needed will be a full canteen. Energy-providing snack foods are also recommended.

For deep adventure, climbing gear such as cord and harnesses will also be required. All schools, outfitters and many clubs can provide this equipment.

If you are interested in purchasing clothing and equipment in Italy, write or call for a free catalog from ILCOM, 14034 Castello d'Annone (Asti), Italy.

Where to Begin

While you can set out to find and explore caves on your own, contacting a local chapter of the CAI will save time and insure the best locations are not overlooked. Because this organization is involved in year-round caving, they can lead you to the local speleology clubs and frequently provide guides and equipment.

Some CAI offices, particularly in the north, have special speleology groups. From these you can obtain detailed maps with exact locations and characteristics of caves. Some CAI chapters also organize group expeditions, spelunking schools and weekend courses. Once you have decided where to begin your adventure, write or call one of the local CAI chapters or the central office (addresses and telephone numbers in Appendix D). Since these offices handle many areas of adventure, be specific with your requests. Tell them when you will be in town, what you would like to do, and what information you need.

Spelunking Schools and Group Expeditions

If you come to Italy without previous spelunking experience, you can still enjoy the country's subterranean beauty through one of the organized school or group expeditions that are formed each year.

By planning in advance, you can attend a week-long school—usually during July—sponsored by the National Speleological Society. This is also a good organization to write for general information on caving in Italy and detailed location maps.

One of nearly 21,000 caves to be explored in Italy.

Contact the Società Speleologica Italiana, Segretaria S. Maccio, Via Gramsci 11, 60035 Jesi Ancona, Italy.

Outfitters in Italy that offer group caving expeditions, training, or a combination of both, include: Special Group Piertoffoletti Production; La Roncola; and Sardegna da Scoprire (addresses can be found in Appendix A).

Favorite Spelunking Sites

Because there are so many caves in Italy, making a selection can be difficult. Italian speleologists, while enjoying a number of sites, note the Antro del Corchia, the Abisso Saragato, the Abisso Roversi, the Grotta di Piaggiabella, the Spluga della Preta, the Abisso Gortani and the caves of Mount Cucco as some of the most popular and exciting excursions for visiting spelunkers.

The following pages provide a brief description of each site. If you are interested in exploring one or more of the sites, a point of contact is also given.

ANTRO DEL CORCHIA

The Antro del Corchia, also known as the Buca d'Eolo, is the largest underground cave network in Tuscany and one of the largest in Italy. Located within Mount Corchia, in the Apuan Alps, the Antro can be entered in 6 locations. Most often used are the Serpente, Buca d'Eolo and Ingressi Alti entrances on the mountain's south side. The entire complex extends over a distance of 3 kilometers and reaches a depth of nearly 1 kilometer.

Those interested in exploring the Antro del Corchia should contact the Gruppo Speleologico Fiorentino at the Florence office of the Italian Alpine Club (address in Appendix D).

ABISSO SARAGATO

The Saragato Abyss is noted for its vertical configuration and its frequent air currents. It is located within Mount Tambura in the central zone of the Apuan Alps. Discovered in 1966 by a

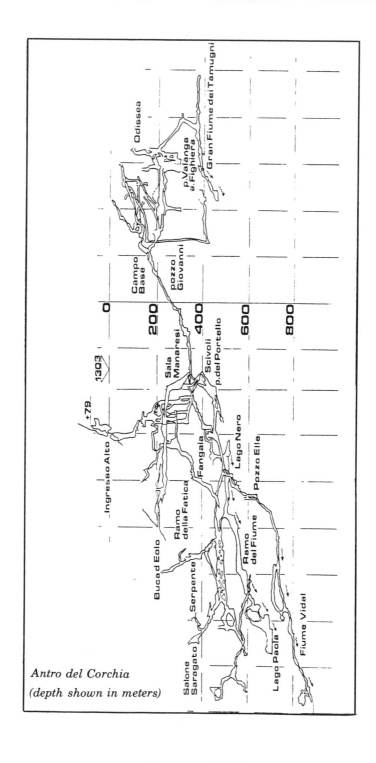

Antro del Corchia
(depth shown in meters)

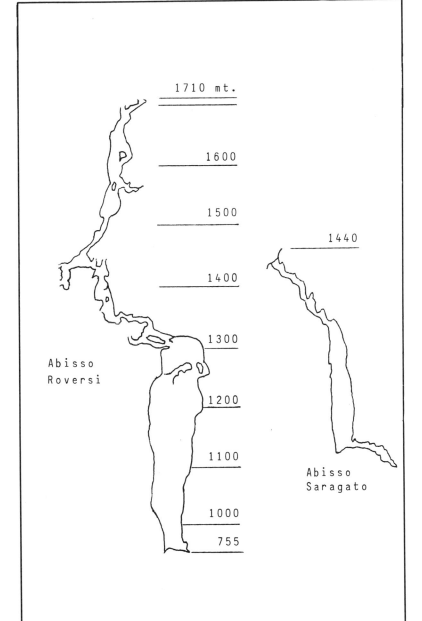

Abisso Saragato and Abisso Roversi
(depth shown in meters)

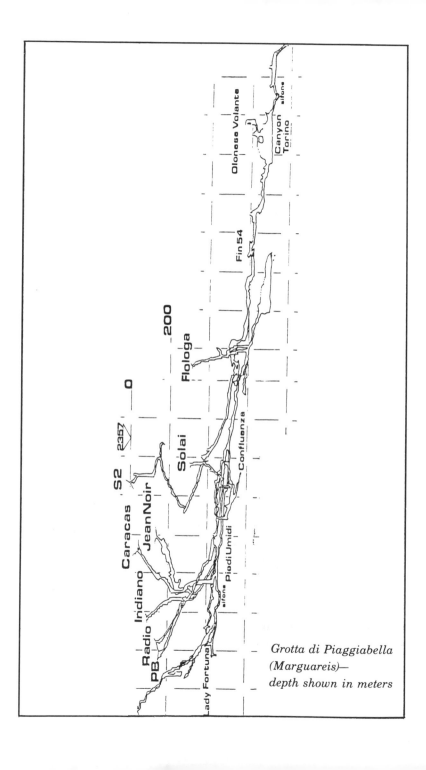

Grotta di Piaggiabella
(Marguareis)—
depth shown in meters

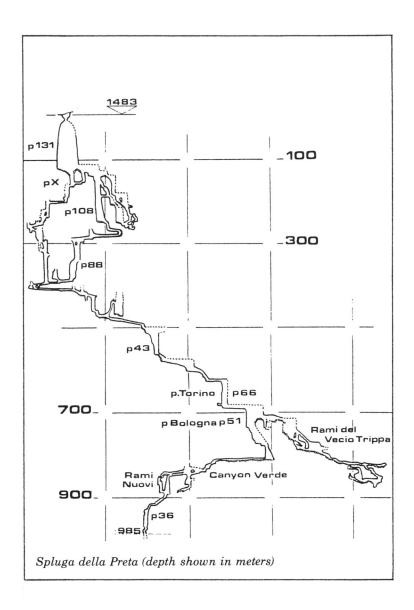

Spluga della Preta (depth shown in meters)

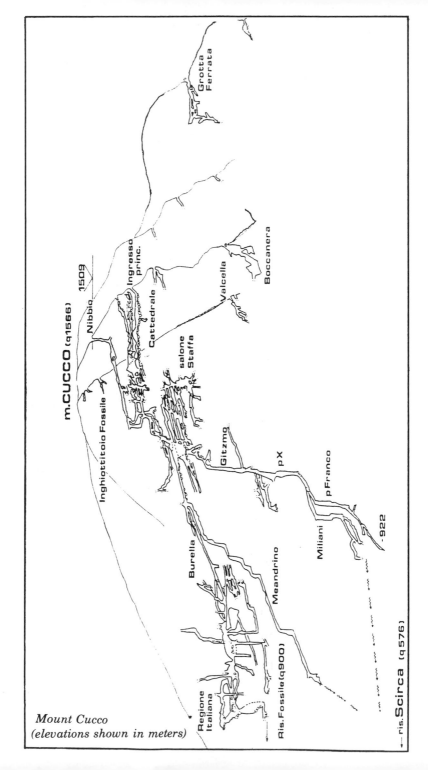

Mount Cucco
(elevations shown in meters)

group of speleologists from Florence, the Saragato opens at an altitude of 1,440 meters and drops 345 meters. While a descent is not too difficult, temperatures can be very cold.

The Saragato Abyss—and the Roversi Abyss, which follows— is situated in the province of Lucca and therefore comes under the jurisdiction of the Italian Alpine Club in that city. However, for speleological outings contact the Florence office, where the local speleological club has its center.

ABISSO ROVERSI

The Abisso Roversi is the deepest and most interesting abyss in Tuscany and perhaps in all of Italy. Like the Saragato, it is located within Mount Tambura. The Roversi Abyss was discovered and first explored in 1977. The entrance at 1,710 feet is relatively small, but expands into larger chambers and an underground system extending 755 meters into the earth.

GROTTA DI PIAGGIABELLA (Marguareis)

The Marguareis mountain range extends along the north of Italy, overlapping the regions of Piedmont and Liguria as well as parts of France. Within this range there are several cave networks. Especially popular among Italian speleologists is the Grotta di Piaggiabella in the province of Cuneo. The network descends nearly 800 meters and extends for 3.6 kilometers. There are several entrances to the Grotta di Piaggiabella, the principle ones situated in the Colle del Pas.

This complex lies within the zone of the Italian Alpine Club of Cuneo. Those interested in making an excursion into the Grotta di Piaggiabella are advised to contact them for more details and to arrange for a guide.

SPLUGA DELLA PRETA

One of the most exciting formations of all Italy, the Spluga della Preta's only entrance is at Corno di Aquilio in the community of San'Anna d'Alfaedo, near Verona. From here, the cave extends nearly 1 kilometer into the earth, branching off in a number of locations, and extending laterally some 500 meters. Though deep, the Spluga della Preta's passages are for the most part extremely large. First explored in 1922, the cave has since been visited by many spelunkers.

For more information, contact the Italian Alpine Club of Verona.

MOUNT CUCCO

Mount Cucco is located near Gubbio in the region of Umbria. Though it resembles many other mountains, speleologists discovered in 1889 that beneath its peak lies a vast network of beautiful caves. Today that cave system has been explored as far down as 1 kilometer. There are two openings to the major networks: the principle entrance at an altitude of 1,375 meters and the Nibbio entrance at 1,509 meters. In the general vicinity there are minor caves as well, such as the Grotta Ferrata and the Boccanera.

Exploring Mount Cucco's cave system is best done with a guide. This can be arranged through the Italian Alpine Club in Perugia.

PART IX

HOT FOOT ADVENTURES

Because of the excitement and obvious danger, volcano exploring has become a favored pastime among thrill-seeking athletes and adventurers in Italy. And with the Mediterranean's underground hot-belt always bubbling up in one place or another, you won't have to go far.

Volcanoes have always inspired awe and wonder. Yet, they are one of nature's simpler phenomena. The earth's core is nothing more than a molten hotbed. From this core, magma (the orange, molten liquid) flows directly to the surface through channels such as Sicily's Mount Etna, which is constantly active. In other cases, magma is stored in chambers that expand below the earth's surface, like a balloon, and eventually erupt. Most volcanoes found in Europe are of the "vent" type, with the expanding gases forming the earth into a cone shape as they are forced out. In such volcanic formations, it is common to see smoke but no magma. This is because the molten lava cools prior to reaching the surface.

Italy's Active Volcanoes

The active volcanoes in Italy—Vesuvius, Vulcano, Stromboli and Etna—stretch along a line which runs almost perfectly north to south below the earth's surface. Although these monsters of nature share characteristics similar to all volcanoes (an underground pocket of magma, a conduit and a cone formed by previous eruptions), their temperaments are neither wholly predictable nor similar.

Vesuvius, which was last active in 1944, has become the European training ground for many explorers. Located 7.5 miles (12 kilometers) south of Naples, the mountain in its present state offers ideal conditions for volcanic studies and stamina conditioning.

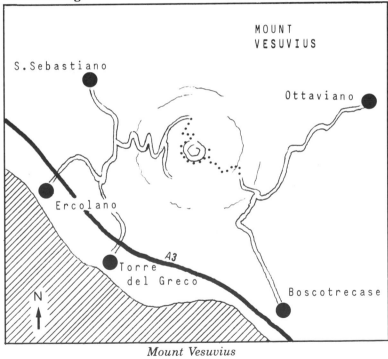

Mount Vesuvius

Mt. Etna at the 8000-foot level.

Vesuvius is also the center of Mediterranean volcanic studies for those interested in the scientific side of exploring and observing the conditions of a volcano. The Osservatoria Vesuviano, established on the mountain's western slopes to monitor geological movements, has assisted many adventurers who have become engrossed in the workings of volcanoes.

The 3,891-foot/1,186-meter peak of Mount Vesuvius can be approached from Portici and Ercolano to the west, Boscoreale to the south and, from the north-west, the town of Ottaviano. Roads from the north, west and south lead up the slopes, ending in parking zones where you must continue on foot. From each location you can walk the rim of the crater and, from the west, a cable-car provides excursions over the gaping chasm.

Volcanic Islands

Located off the north-eastern coast of Sicily in the archipelago of the Aeolian or Lipari Islands, Stromboli has been active since the beginning of recorded time. Like Vesuvius, it rises in a single cone formation, currently reaching 3,038 feet (926 meters). Moving around this smoking island-volcano is relatively easy for explorers. It does, however, present certain dangers, as do all volcanoes. In this case, awesome crevasses such as the Sciarra del Fuoco (Pit of Fire), where lava flows can be observed, should be approached with extreme caution.

Hiking to the summit of Stromboli along well-travelled paths, takes about 3 hours.

Another of the Aeolian Islands that draws volcano explorers is Vulcano. This, the closest island to Sicily, is a smoking mass of lava rising to 1,637 feet (504 meters). Though steam and gas are always present, the last true eruption of Vulcano was in 1890. From the town of Gran Cratere, there is a road that will take you part-way up the mountain or, if you prefer, you can make the venture on foot. A climb to the volcanic crater takes about 1 hour from the eastern harbor.

To get to Stomboli and Vulcano, as well as other Aeolian Islands, catch one of the boats which depart daily from Milazzo, on the north-eastern coast of Sicily.

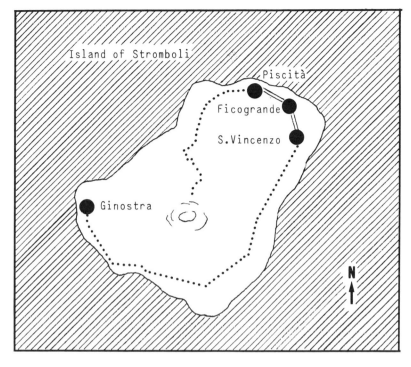

Stromboli

Etna

One of the principal active volcanoes in the world, the largest in Europe, Etna has been recorded for centuries as a fire-spitting cone of fearsome splendor. When lava is flowing, Etna illuminates the Sicilian landscape, and on a clear day it can be seen from a distance of 150 miles.

Though it is always active, a tremendous eruption took place in early 1983 when Etna's molten lava and gas sent frightened inhabitants of isolated centers fleeing down the mountainside with whatever possessions they could gather. What followed was the largest flow of molten lava from the volcano in 20 years. Thick, dark smoke and ashes bellowed into the sky as the cork burst from the mountaintop, releasing the fury that

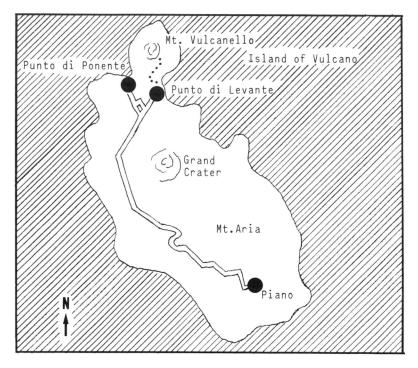

Vulcano

had been contained for so long. With each thundering burst, fiery ash was spewed over the volcano's slopes.

Since historic records began, there have been more than 150 such eruptions from Etna. These have resulted in a volcanic mountain with a base circumference of 125 miles (201 kilometers) and an altitude of 11,000 feet (3,352 meters). This height varies, however, according to the area that one explores.

Today, Etna is constantly bubbling in one or more of its many craters. It is probably as close to a vision of hell as any mortal is likely to get. Because of this, the mountain has been rated highly on adventurers' lists. You have to respect the mountain, however. It can be threatening and even dangerous under certain conditions. If not approached with extreme caution and common sense in the area of volcanic activities, a real danger exists.

Etna lights up the night sky with belching lava.

From the cities of Catania or Taormina, Etna can be reached by bus or car. A road from the town of Nicolosi leads to the Rifugio Sapienza on the mountain's southern slopes. Here the SITAS organization operated a cable car which took visitors up Etna until 1985. During that year a lava flow destroyed part of the cable-way making it inoperative.

From this 6,309-foot/1,923-meter level, adventurers can now take mountain buses to 10,072 feet (3,070 meters), a drive which takes about 45 minutes. Here, guides accompany visitors to the summit craters which are often flowing with hot lava and/or spewing towards the sky with lion-like roars.

You can also walk to the upper levels of Mount Etna, though the best way to see the surrounding territory is to ride the buses up, then return by walking the 7.5 miles (12 kilometers) down to the landing station. By doing so you will get a true feel for Etna and its activity. Many past lava flows are marked with the dates, some as far back as the 1700s. Walking down

217

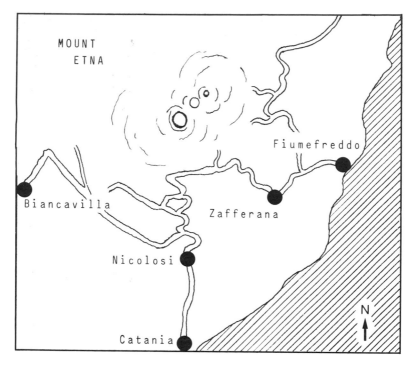

Etna

the mountain will also allow you to view the enormous Val del Bove on the south-east slopes.

Despite the ever-present, 1,300° F (704° C) lava flows, Etna is a seasonal adventure. Most explorers make the trip between May and October. This is also when the busses operate. The rest of the year the summit is often buried in snow.

A trek up Etna, Stromboli, Vulcano or, for that matter, even Vesuvius, is a personal adventure. The slopes are not patrolled in most cases, adding even more excitement—and risk.

Safety, conditioning and proper gear are essential factors in volcano exploring. Even in the height of summer, the higher levels of most volcanoes can be very cold. Etna, for example, often has winds up to 100 knots or more, which add to the chill factor. In months other than summer, temperatures can be extremely bitter. The greater altitudes, more often than not, are shrouded in clouds and visibility can be poor.

Rugged shoes and clothing are a must in any season, though especially so if you plan a long stay at higher levels. Water should be included on the necessity list: the climb will be dehydrating.

Volcano exploring is really no more dangerous than mountain climbing, but when the ground thunders beneath your feet and a lump of hot rock shoots a half-mile into the sky, you'll feel a thrill—if you want to call it that—no other adventure can provide.

Gearing Up for Volcanic Adventures

Like any sport, volcano exploring requires some special gear. While you might already have much of the necessary equipment, particularly if you are into hiking or mountain climbing, there are a few items that could easily be overlooked.

Boots are number 1 on the list. There are a number of good brands, but the key factor is to have thick leather soles. Many people have made the mistake of using boots with rubber or plastic soles on the slopes of Etna. This frequently results in hot feet and, in some cases, melted soles.

Heavy socks, long pants, long underwear, coat, hat, gloves and sunglasses should be seriously considered, particularly for excursions up Etna. It may seem ridiculous to bundle up when the weather at the mountain base is sunny and mild, but once you get into higher altitudes you will be glad to have the extra clothing.

A walking stick is very useful when it comes to stepping along hazardous areas. A light aluminum stick is best.

A full canteen of water is another must, even for short excursions. You will not find any water holes on volcanoes.

Because of the natural beauty volcanic environments provide, a camera is often appreciated by hot-foot explorers. Some of the most dramatic images ever captured on film have come from sudden lava bursts.

Though you may never need to use it, a first-aid kit should be taken for all outings.

Most of these items will easily fit into a backpack. If you decide to camp on a volcano, which is frequently done—though sites must be selected with great care—you will also want to include the usual camping gear.

One thing not found in sporting goods stores, but very important: a medical mask. You've probably seen them worn by doctors and nurses in operating rooms. These came in handy if you are exploring an active volcano that has sulfur fumes seeping from its crevasses. If you know someone who works in a hospital or even a dentist, they could probably pick up one or two of these for you. They can also be purchased inexpensively at medical supply houses. Or ask your local doctor.

Hiking on Mt. Etna.

Practical Information

Maps and general information on Italy's volcanoes can be obtained by writing the tourist boards in the regions where the volcanoes are located (addresses are found in Appendix C). In addition, you can write or visit the following provincial tourist offices: (for Mount Vesuvius) Azienda Autonoma di Cura, Soggiorno e Turismo di Napoli, Via Partenope 10a, 80100 Naples, Italy; (for Mount Etna) Ente Provinciale per il Turismo, Largo Paisiello 5, 95124 Catania, Italy or the Azienda Autonoma di Cura, Soggiorno e Turismo, Corso Umberto 179, 95024 Acireale, Italy; (for the Aeolian Island volcanoes) Ente Provinciale per il Turismo, Via Calabria is. 301/bis, 98100 Messina, Italy or the Azienda Autonoma Soggiorno e Turismo, Corso Vittorio Emanuele 239, 98055 Lipari, Italy.

Another means of obtaining maps, information and guides to the volcanoes of Sicily, particularly Mount Etna, is through the Italian Alpine Club of Catania (address in Appendix D).

PART X

ARCHAEOLOGICAL EXPEDITIONS

Hundreds of non-experts participate in archaeological digs throughout Italy each year. For many, these are once-in-a-lifetime experiences. Whether one uncovers great treasures or not, archaeological adventures provide excitement and an education.

Because of Italy's rich history, archaeological remains can be found nearly everywhere, including most of the islands. This over-abundance of sites has imposed a burden on the limited funds provided by the government for excavation. One of the major problems, therefore, is selecting the most important sites to dig. This, however, is realistically impossible. After all, who is to say that a tiny, out-of-the-way site may not hold one of the greatest discoveries of all time while digs in well-known areas such as Pompeii might prove completely fruitless?

For these reasons, the Italians welcome outside assistance which enables them to explore more sites.

Many adventurers have discovered that you don't have to be an archaeologist, historian, or scientist to participate in such activities. Men and women 16 to 75—school teachers, business people, doctors, students, engineers, retired persons—have volunteered their assistance and shared in the endeavor of learning more about the peninsula.

Getting in on an archaeological dig such as this is not as difficult as many believe.

How do you become a member of an archaeological expedition in Italy?

One of he best ways is through universities that offer summer fieldwork opportunities. Each year there are hundreds of such projects. Recently, for instance, the Archaeology Department of the Rhode Island School of Design, offered 18 students and amateur archaeologists the opportunity to study and work at various digs in Rome. Sheffield University of England sponsored a 2-month project for volunteers in Molise, Italy. At a site outside Rome, Ithaca College of New York brought in archaeological buffs for a week-long excavation. On the island of Sardinia, several teams from the University of California have been digging up past civilizations while the University of Texas is concentrating on the Neolithic, Bronze, Greek, Roman, and Medieval periods of Metaponta and Croton, with a team consisting of a staff photographer and 6 volunteers.

The fact that many digs are sponsored by colleges does not necessarily mean that you must be a student to get involved. According to a representative of the University of California's University Research Expeditions Program (UREP), no special academic or field experience is necessary for most expeditions. A desire to learn and willingness to work and share the costs are essential. Flexibility, being a team member, and adaptability to new and challenging situations are important too.

Like UREP, more and more archaeological expeditions are being funded by the participants. Because of this, you may find your participation in such adventures costing as much as $2000. At the same time, there are those that can be enjoyed for as little as $50 per week, including food and lodging. In many cases, these expenses go to supporting the actual expedition and are, therefore, tax deductable.

There are also agencies, other than colleges and universities, that sponsor archaeological expeditions to Italy each year. One such operation is Earthwatch. Recently, Earthwatch volunteers uncovered 8,000-year-old remnants of Neolithic farmers in Lucera, Italy, with anthropologist Daniel Evett. This was but one of more than 20 archaeological ventures organized by the Massachusetts-based company to support the efforts of scholars. To date, Earthwatch, a non-profit organization founded in 1971, has sponsored 730 projects in 68 countries, providing researchers with nearly 15,000 volunteers and more than $8 million in funds and equipment.

One of the hardest parts of becoming an archaeological team member, so it would seem, is discovering who to contact for information on available expeditions, their costs, dates, and procedures for application. The Archaeological Institute of America (P.O. Box 1901, Kenmore Station, Boston, Massachusetts 02215) has solved that problem with an annual "Archaeological Fieldwork Opportunities Bulletin." A recent edition lists more than 140 archaeological adventures throughout the world, as well as some basic information on joining expeditions, and a listing of over 200 sources for further information.

Archaeological fieldwork is exciting, romantic and a time for intellectual and personal growth. But it also is physically demanding and tedious: it requires patience, flexibility and enthusiasm. Italy is one country where that patience can be well rewarded.

Digging for More Information

There are several places where you can begin your quest for archaeological adventure in Italy. Organizations such as the University Research Expeditions Program and Earthwatch (addresses can be found in Appendix A) are a good first step.

There are also archaeological clubs in Italy that arrange several digs each summer: Gruppi Archeologici d'Italia, Via Tacito 41, Rome, Italy; and the Archeoclub d'Italia, Arco de'Banchi 8, Rome, Italy. Writing these organizations is an excellent way to obtain information and get involved. The fact that you may not speak or write Italian is normally no barrier.

PART XI

MORE ADVENTURES

In addition to hiking, biking, canoeing, caving, volcano exploring and archaeological adventures, Italy offers such activities as diving, ultra-light flying, horseback trekking, sled dog racing, gold hunting and even survival schools. For those who would like to pursue one of these, the following chapter will be of particular interest.

Underwater Adventures

Italy is an ideal place for underwater adventures that can bring you face-to-face with easily accessible remnants of past civilizations, as well as plant and animal life unknown to most divers.

Much of what you will want to see underwater in Italy, is found in water less than 20 feet deep, so it can be enjoyed equally by snorklers and scuba enthusiasts. Water temperatures are relatively mild throughout the year, particularly in the southern regions. From June through October snorklers will normally not require a wetsuit. During other months of the year, or for deeper scuba activities, some form of outer protection is required.

The Mediterranean is an excellent place for underwater archaeology. It is not uncommon to find ancient foundations or other evidence of past civilizations buried among shifting sands. Off the shores of Pozzuoli and Sperlonga, on the southwestern coast of the peninsula, in roughly 12 feet of water, lie the ruins of what were once prosperous Roman ports. Italian law prohibits the removal of antiquities from the sea; however, it does provide a monetary compensation for major discoveries.

Spearfishing is normally excellent around Sicily and Sardinia, as well as most of the lower regions. In addition to fish, there are octopus, dark bivalved mussels, clams, shrimp and the Mediterranean lobster, which is a bit smaller but just as good to eat as its American cousin.

Underwater fishing can be pursued only without the use of respiratory equipment. Law permits the use of such equipment only for motives other than fishing.

For those who know what they're doing, caves can be explored around the islands of Sicily, Capri, and on much of the Calabrian coast. This type of adventure, however, calls for experience, proper equipment, and a reliable diving partner.

Unlike most of the world's water bodies, the Mediterranean contains very few dangers. Rarely does one come across sharks or more threatening creatures than jellyfish, eels and numerous urchins. Those who have some experience with salt water diving will, therefore, find this sea a relaxing paradise of both natural splendor and safety. When diving near the shore, you should be alert to the possible hazard of fishing nets, however.

To fill scuba tanks in Italy you must present a diver's certification card. The most noted certifying agency in Italy is PADI, though some others exist. Unlike the United States and many other countries, Italian law requires that tanks be hydrostatically tested every 2 years and be stamped with the testing date. Tanks that have not been tested within this period will not be filled by commercial air stations. In addition, divers caught diving with expired hydro test dates face a fine and the confiscation of their equipment.

Diving flags are mandatory in Italy.

Most of Italy's underwater attractions can be found in water less than 20 feet deep.

FINDING A DIVING PARTNER

Because there is a high concentration of American and NATO military in Italy, it is not difficult to find English-speaking divers. In Naples you can contact NATO's Sub Aqua Club (Allied Forces Southern Europe, Box 141, FPO New York, NY 09524). Club members, consisting primarily of American and British military, organize weekend dives, fill tanks, and have a limited selection of rental equipment. Similar clubs, affiliated with the U.S. military, can be found in Sigonella, Sicily (Mediterranean Divers Club, USNAS Sigonella, FPO New York, NY 09523), and Vicenza, in north-central Italy (Vicenza Dive Club, HHC, USMCAV, CSMA, APO New York, NY 09221; also Aquaknights of Atlantis, 1605 Air Base Wing, APO New York, NY 09406).

Italian dive clubs are located in major cities throughout the country. One that has established a reputation for hosting for-

Mediterranean diving can be safer and more relaxing than ocean diving.

eign divers is the Centro d'Immersione di Sorrento (Parco Nizza 71, 80067 Sorrento, Italy). In addition to weekly dives, this club has an annual Christmas dive in the Grotta Esmeralda, off the coast of Amalfi, where a lighted, underwater nativity scene has been placed. The holiday dive has become famous throughout the world and is visited by hundreds of divers each year.

High-flying Adventure

One of the fastest growing adventure sports in Italy is free flying with ultra-light craft and parachutes.

Unlike the parachutes used for jumps from planes at high altitudes and speeds of 140 miles per hour, adventurers enjoying the thrill of this sport use open hang-chutes and take running leaps from mountain peaks. Ultra-light gliders and motorized delta planes are also used by many.

Because much of Italy is mountainous, free flying is done in many areas. The Apennine mountain range in the province of Perugia, is a preferred site, particularly the peaks around the towns of Castelluccio, Norcia and Arquata del Tronto. Here one also finds the Deltaflying School and Polaris, a well-known manufacturer of flying craft and parachutes.

In addition to instructions, the Deltaflying School offers rental equipment, guides and visitor assistance. The personnel of the school can point out the best sites and often include you in upcoming group outings.

Another group that is doing much for Italy in the area of free flying is the Centro Volo Libero Etna Delta on the island of Sicily. In addition to running the Scuola Italiana Volo Libero (Italian School of Free Flying), the center offers delta glider planes, motorized delta planes and hang-parachutes. Also available are 15-day tours of Sicily with flights from the island's most noted locations. Though the center operates offices in Taormina, Palermo, Caltagirone and Siracusa, its headquarters is in the province of Catania.

For more details on free flying in Italy, write: Deltaflying, Via Flaminia 208, 06021, Costacciaro (PG), Italy; or Centro

Ultra-light craft in flight.

Volo Libero Etna Delta, Via Diana 124, 95013 Fiumefreddo di Sic. (CT), Italy. The latter organization can also provide information on the Federazione Italiana Volo Libero (Italian Free Flying Federation).

Dog Sled School

"Iditarod," the most famous dog-sled race in the world, is held each year is Alaska. The race covers a 1,049-mile trail from Anchorage to Nome. Until recently only one Italian had ever competed in the Iditarod. Now, however, "mushers" from the Bianca Sledog School in northern Italy are striving to win this epic course. In fact, under the Bianca banner a team led by Rick Swenson, 4-time winner of the Iditarod, now races.

Throughout Germany, Switzerland, Austria and now Italy, many spectacular races are being organized and the number of participants is increasing steadily.

For all people who are keen to try this exciting new sport, the Bianca Sledog School in Ponte di Legno-Tonale (Lombardy Region) is a good place to start. They offer 1-week packages which include hotel accommodations on a half-board basis, 18 hours of theoretical and practical dog sledding lessons, a card for free use of skiing facilities, transfer to and from the dog sled school and a race at the end of the course. Dogs and equipment are provided by the school and each participant also receives a sled dog manual.

During the summer the courses are given on the Adamello glacier and include downhill and cross-country skiing, rock climbing and first-aid as well. All instructors have been trained by American champion Rick Swenson, who is acting director of the school. In the summer program accommodations are in an Alpine refuge and transfer to the glacier is by helicopter.

For a free packet of information, including application forms

For those seeking a different kind of adventure, sled dog schools can be found in Northern Italy.

233

and fees, write: Azienda Autonoma di Soggiorno, 25056 Ponte di Legno, Italy; or Bianca, Viale Pasubio 6, 20154 Milan, Italy.

Horseback Trekking

Throughout Italy people are taking to horseback trekking. During the summer and fall—and at other times of the year—individuals can be found enjoying horseback excursions along beaches, wooded trails, dried river beds, open meadows and even through the Alps. Horseback trekking requires little physical energy and is an excellent way to enjoy the country's natural beauty. The regions of Piedmont, Lombardy, Veneto, Emilia, Tuscany, Umbria, Abruzzo, Lazio, Sardinia and Sicily are extremely popular for outings of this type.

There are currently about 300 centers for horseback vacations. Of these nearly 25% specialize in nature trips, offering not only the animals for transportation but all the necessary equipment, including camping gear and/or accommodations along the trail as well as food. Most often these treks are limited to those 14 years of age and over. Typical horseback trips last 7–10 days, covering 22 miles (35 kilometers) each day. There are also a few outfitters that offer weekend adventures. The cost ranges from 500,000 to 800,000 lire for 1- and 2-week ventures. Weekend treks begin at 200,000 lire.

For more information on horseback adventures, write to the Associazione Nazionale Turismo Equestre (ANTE) Largo Messico 13, 00198 Roma. (See Appendix A for outfitters offering horseback nature tours.)

Survival Schools

Over the past decade outdoor survival schools have boomed in Italy. Many of these began as a result of the Rambo craze that swept Europe a few years back. Most of the fly-by-night outfits have since faded and what remains are a number of serious schools where one learns the techniques of living off the land

and, not incidentally, a deeper understanding of the natural environment.

There is a personal satisfaction involved in attending an outdoor survival school that is difficult to explain. Despite what many think, the hardest part is often overcoming your fears and building self confidence. The key to wilderness survival according to most instructors, in fact, is in having the will to meet every challenge.

Whether the obstacle is a river, a mountain, a swamp, or merely starting a fire without matches or a lighter, no one is forced. If you feel unable to perform a certain task, you are encouraged to try. If unsuccessful, you are not shunned, ridiculed, or turned away. You are part of a team; and the team's mission is to survive as well as learn.

Most schools place a great emphasis on nature studies. You learn to cope with the natural environment and take advantage of it. Food, water, shelter, fire and most other needs can all be satisfied by nature, if you only know where to look and how to obtain them.

While conducted in different locations and under different circumstances, most Italian survival schools teach similar skills. These include the construction of natural shelters, obtaining food and water supplies, starting fires, techniques in climbing, building of water crafts and utilizing rivers for transportation, traversing rivers and canyons via rope cords, methods for crossing swamps, and finding your way with and without the use of a compass.

Some schools also include speleology, archery and firearm training in their curriculums. The Special Group Piertoffoletti of Udine combines all of these elements into a 15-day course of outdoor education and living.

"We don't like to use the world 'survival'," says Pier Carlo Toffoletti, director of the Special Group. "It is just too big a word. It is probably more accurate to say that we teach wilderness environment adaptability."

The only enrollment restriction maintained by most schools is a minimum age limit of 16. Naturally you must also be in fair physical condition, but it is not uncommon to find "students" in the 40–50 year range. There are also a growing number of women who undertake these adventurous classes.

For those in search of more, some survival schools offer advanced and special training. The Italian Association for Survival Education, for example, offers a number of organized schools, including a 5-day mountain survival course held each summer in collaboration with the Italian Alpine Club of Turin. Jacek Palkiewicz's "Scuola di Sopravvivenza" frequently runs specifically designed courses in such areas as open water and jungle survival.

Seasonal courses are also offered. At the Survival High School in Vicenza, one can learn not only general wilderness survival, but winter, desert, and river survival training.

Survival schools teach climbing techniques and other outdoor skills.

Because most of the country's survival schools are conducted in the Italian language, the Survival High School has become a favorite among English-speaking adventurers for the mere fact that it has courses in their mother tongue.

Addresses for Italy's survival schools can be found in Appendix A.

Going For Gold

To say that there is a "gold rush" going on in Italy would be a slight exaggeration. To say that many adventurers have found gold, and that some even make a good living prospecting during the summer months, would be more accurate. It all started around 1980 when travelers to the northern region of Piedmont began finding glittering chips in local rivers. These chips, as it turned out, were flakes of gold. By 1985, gold finds were at such a level that the "World Gold Panning Championship" was held in the city of Ovada, the center of Italy's gold belt.

While gold is being found today in many parts of the Piedmont and Liguria regions, the most prosperous areas have proven to be among the rocks of Monte Rosa and the Gran Paradiso, as well as the streams of Piota, Lemme, Gorzente, Borberu, and Siura. Much success has also been reported along the Orco, Elba, Elvo, Ticini and Orba rivers. In fact, any of the streams in the Val d'Ossola, the Valley of Bognanco, the Valley Anzasca, and the valley of Orco are worth trying.

Recent finds have proven that Piedmont and Liguria are not the only regions that offer gold, however. Other streams which have brought success include: the Taro, the Panaro, the Secchia and the Enza, in Emilia; in Tuscany, the Serchio, the Paglia, and the area around Monte Amiata; and, in Calabria, the Esaro and the tributaries of the Allaro.

For more information on gold hunting in Italy, including maps of the most productive areas, contact the Associazione Cercatori d'Oro, c/o Consorzio Turistico Ovadese, Via Torino 65, 15076 Ovada (AL), Italy. For 5,000 lire, or equivalent in foreign currency, you can become a member of the association, which entitles you to a membership card, club sticker, and newsletter that includes national and international information on gold hunting.

For those who know nothing about gold panning but have a desire to give it a try, the association also operates 8-day courses, in collaboration with Teknogeo and the Silvano d'Orbo City Hall, beginning in June and running through October.

APPENDIX A

OUTFITTERS

Alabirdi
Strada a mare 24
09021 Arborea (Oristano), Italy

Tel: (0783) 48268 or 48512

One of the finest outfitters for horseback vacations on the island of Sardinia. Outings are arranged along the beaches as well as internally.

Associazione Ciao & Basta
Costa dei Magnoli 24
50125 Florence, Italy

Organizer of bicycle tours and itineraries, particularly in the region of Tuscany.

Associazione per l'Educazione alla Sopravvivenza
Via Priocca, 30
10152 Torino, Italy

Tel: (011) 822–5394

Courses in mountain survival are conducted by this outfit each summer, normally between June and September.

Cap Horse
06073 Capocavallo di Corciana (PG)
Italy

Tel: (075) 605–858 or 605–705

Organized week-long horseback trekking in the Umbria region. A good natural setting.

Centro Ippico Fattoria del Cerreto
Abruzzo Mosciano S. Angelo
64023 (Teramo) Italy

Tel: (085) 863–806 or 864–076

Week-long or weekend horseback trekking in the Abruzzo region.

Club Avventour
Via dei Campani 63
00185 Rome, Italy

Tel: (06) 495–8249

This operation provides week-long canoe trips on the island of Sardinia, complete with transportation, camping facilities and equipment.

Earthwatch
10 Juniper Road
Box 127
Belmont, Massachusetts 02178

Tel: (617) 489–3030

Earthwatch supports the efforts of scholars to preserve the world's endangered habitats and species, explores the vast heritage of its people, and promotes world health and international cooperation. They regularly organize archaeological and other expeditions to Italy.

Gruppo Trekking Firenze
Piazza S. Gervasio, 12
Florence, Italy 50131

Tel: (055) 55–320

Trekking ventures in Tuscany are the specialty of this group. They offer several itineraries, week-long or weekend excursions.

Hiking International
1–3 George Street
Oxford OX1 2AZ, England

Tel: (0865) 251195/6

One of the top English-language outfitters for group and independent adventures. Hiking International offers a vast selection of walking, trekking, bicycling, and canoing activities in Italy, including horseback adventures.

Il Tucano
Viaggi Ricerca di Willy Fassio & Co.
Via Cernaia, 3
10121 Torino, Italy

Tel: (011) 548–173 or 510–979

Trekking adventures in Piedmont, Val d'Aosta and Sicily (Mount Etna) stressing local flora and fauna, getting in touch with nature as well as some historical tourism.

La Roncola
Via Nazionale, 4
50123 Florence, Italy

Tel: (055) 229–8289

Formed in 1983, La Roncola organizes treks in the Dolomites, bicycle tours from Ravenna among the marches of the Po, Alpine canyon descents and camping ventures, canoe trips throughout the country, speleological trips, and hiking trips. They work regularly with English-speaking groups.

Rentola Riding
52020 Rentola Valdarno (AR)
Italy

Tel: (055) 987–045

Horseback trekking in the beautiful region of Tuscany.

Sardegna da Scoprire
Via Dante, 29
08100 Nuoro, Italy

Tel: (0784) 304–00

Organizers of week-long speleology adventures on the island of Sardinia, including training, gear, and descents.

Special Group Piertoffoletti
Via Luccardi, 41
33100 Udine, Italy

Tel: (0432) 602–641

Special Group Piertoffoletti organizes mountain treks, free climbing, spelunking and survival school adventures. They offer each activity separately or in the form of a 15-day experience which includes each activity (from June-September).

Survival High School
c/o Massimo Canevarolo
Casella Postale 474
36100 Vicenza, Italy

Tel: (0444) 568–8009

A year-round survival school which offers courses in English.

Tenuta la Mandria
13062 Candelo (VC)
Italy

Tel: (015) 53078

Horseback adventures, including weekend and week-long trekking in the region of Piedmont.

Trekking International
Corso Sempione, 60
20154 Milan, Italy

Tel: (02) 318-9161

Trekking International, one of the best-known outfitters of mountain treks, countryside hikes, horseback adventures, and volcano exploring, deals regularly with English-speaking groups. Most adventures organized by Trekking International take place from June to October.

University Research Expeditions Program (UREP)
University of California
Berkeley, CA 94720

Tel: (415) 642-6586

UREP sponsors archaeological digs in Italy that are supported and carried out by volunteers.

Valsesia Adventure School
Protur-Valsesia
P.O. Box 1316
13019 Varallo Sesia (VC), Italy

The Valsesia Adventure School offers individual adventures such as hiking, canoing, mountain climbing, and speleology or a combination of these in one package. They also offer organized survival courses, which incorporate many of the above activities.

APPENDIX B

USEFUL TELEPHONE NUMBERS

APPENDIX C

REGIONAL TOURIST BOARDS

ABRUZZI: Via Bovio, 65100 Pescara, Italy.
APUGLIA: Via Capruzzi 212, 70100 Bari, Italy.
BASILICATA: Rione Addone, 85100 Potenza, Italy.
CALABRIA: Vico III Raffaelli, 88100 Catanzaro, Italy.
CAMPANIA: Via Santa Lucia 81, 80100 Naples, Italy.
EMILIA ROMAGNA: Viale Silvani 6, 40122 Bologna, Italy.
FRIULI-VENETIA GIULIA: Via G. Rossini 6, 34132 Trieste, Italy.
LATIUM: Via Rosa Raimondi Garibaldi 7, 00100 Rome, Italy.
LIGURIA: Via Fieschi 15, 16121 Genoa, Italy.
LOMBARDY: Via Luigi Sturzo 37, 20100 Milan, Italy.
MOLISE: Via Mazzini 94, 86100 Campobasso, Italy.
PIEDMONT: Via Magenta 12, 10100 Turin, Italy.
SARDINIA: Via Mameli 97, 09100 Cagliari, Italy.
SICILY: Via E. Notarbartolo 9/B, 90141 Palermo, Italy.
MARCHE: Via Gentile da Fabriano, 60100 Ancona, Italy.
TUSCANY: Via Farini 8, 50100 Florence, Italy.
TRENTINO-ALTO ADIGE: (Provincia Autonoma di Trento) Corso III Novembre 132, 38100 Trento, Italy. (Provincia Autonoma di Bolzano) Pfarrplatz 11–12, 39100 Bolzano, Italy.

UMBRIA: Corso Vannucci, Palazzo Donini, 06100 Perugia, Italy.

AOSTA VALLEY: Piazza Narbonne 3, 11100 Aosta, Italy.

VENETO: Palazzo Baldi Dorsoduro 3901, 30100 Venice, Italy.

APPENDIX D

ITALIAN ALPINE CLUBS

The Italian Alpine Club (CAI) has 395 chapters throughout Italy. The following list includes only those found in major cities. If needed, these offices can put you in contact with smaller provincial groups.

For a complete listing of CAI chapters, as well as general information on the organization's activities, contact the national headquarters at Via Ugo Foscolo 3, 20121 Milan, Italy.

The CAI chapters below are listed by location, street address, person in charge, and postal code. When corresponding, use the following address format: (example is for Alessandria) Guido Barberis, Italian Alpine Club, via Venezia 7, 15100 Alessandria, Italy.

Alessandria—via Venezia 7 (Guido Barberis), 15100
Ancono—via Cialdi 29 A/B (Pietro Pazzaglia), 60121
Aosta—piazza Chanoux 8 (Domenico Chatrian), 11100
Arezzo—via San Giovanni Decollato 37 (Raoul De Sanctis), 52100
Ascoli Piceno—corso Massini 81 (Alberico Alesi), 63100
Asti—corso della Vittoria 50 (Fulvio Ercole), 14100
Bari—C.P. 530 (Pietro Tosoni), 70100
Belluno—via Ricci 1 (Roberto Cielo), 32100

Bergamo—via Ghislanzoni 15 (Antonio Salvi), 24100

Bologna—via Indipendenza 2 (Luigi Selleri), 40121

Bolzano—piazza Delle Erbe 46 (Andrea Maria Nesler), 39100

Brescia—piazza Vescovato 3 (Sam Quillieri), 25100

Cagliari—via Principe Amedeo, 25 (Angelo Berio), 09100

Campobasso—via Cardarelli 59 (Antonio Venditti), 86100

Catania—via Vecchia Ognina 169 (Vincenzo Tomasello), 95128

Chieti—via Arniense 119 (Riccardo D'Angelo), 66100

Como—via Volta 56 (Rino Zocchi), 22100

Cremona—corso Garibaldi 112/b (Attilio Rossi), 26100

Cuneo—via Allione 1 (Elio Allario), 12100

Ferrara—via Cairoli 44 (Alessandro Gorini), 44100

Florence—via del Proconsolo 10 (Ugo Bertocchini), 50122

Forlì—via Biondo Flavio 4 (Piero Marconi), 47100

Frosinone—via San Simenone 5 (Sandro Vona), 03100

Genoa-Ligure—piazza Luccoli 2/5 (Roberto Nam), 16123

Grosseto—via Trieste 9, c/o Aloisi, 58100

Imperia-Oneglia—piazza U. Calvi (Luigi Masserini), 18100

L'Aquila—c/o geom. Nanni, via XX Settembre 99 (Nestore Nanni), 67100

La Spezia—via Carpenino 43 C.P. 218 (Enzo Pennacchi), 19100

Latina—via Don Morosini 87 (Guglielmo Andreani), 04100

Livorno—via E. Rossi 24-Terr. (Ferdinando Bastianelli), 57100

Lucca—Palazzo Provinciale, cortile Carrara 18 (Umberto Giannini), 55100

Macerata—piazza Vittorio Veneto (Giuseppe Bommarito), 04100

Mantova—via dei Lattonai 1, Pal. del Podestà (Bruno Fin), 46100

Massa—piazza Mazzini 13 C.P. 109 (Domenico Mignani), 54100

Messina—via Natoli 20 (Ottavio Stracuzzi), 98100

Milan—via Silvio Pellico 6 (Angelo Brambilla), 20121

Modena—via Caselline 11 (Angelo Testoni), 41100

Naples—Castel dell'Ovo (Alfonso Piciocchi), 80132

Novara—via F. Cavallotti 11 (Sandro Silvestri), 28100

Padova—Galleria S. Biagio 5, int. 10 (Livio Grazian), 35100

Palermo—via Agrigento 30 (Nazzareno Rovella), 90141

Parma—via Ospizi Civili 6 (Francesco Terzi), 43100

Pavia—piazza Castello 28 (Cesare Turri), 27100

Perugia—C.P. 329 via della Gabbia 9 (Giancarlo Orzella), 06100

Pesaro—via Bramante 21 (Luigi Perugini), 61100

Pescara—piazza S. Cuore 4 (Franco Rocchetti), 65100

Piacenza—via San Vincenzo 2 (Piero Cappellini), 56100

Pisa—via Cisanello 4 (Alberto Carmellini), 56100

Pistoia—via XXVII Aprile C.P. 1 (Giuseppe Arcangeli), 51100

Pordenone—via Odorico, cond. Ariston (Antonio Bosso), 33170

Ravenna—via Castel San Pietro 28 (Mario Beghi), 48100

Reggio Calabria—C.P. 60 (Franco Cuzzocrea), 89100

Reggio Emilia—corso Garibaldi 14 (Amos Borghi), 42100

Rieti—via Pennina 28 (Alberto Bianchetti), 02100

Rome—via Repetta 142 (Bruno Delisi), 00186

Rovigo—piazza Caffaratti 9-c (Tullio Fabbron), 45100

Savona—piazza Diaz Teatro Chiabrera C.P. 232 (Franco Pecorella), 17100

Siena—via di Città 25 (Umberto Vivi), 53100

Sondrio—via Trieste 27 (Stefano Tirinzoni), 23100

Teramo—via N. Sauro 46 C.P. Aperta (Aldo Possenti), 64100

Terni—c/o C. Coletti, via Roma 96 (Pier Luigi Salustri), 05100

Torino—via Barbaroux 1 (Pier Lorenzo Alvigini), 10122

Treviso—piazza del Signori 4 (Roberto Galanti), 31100

Trieste—via Machiavelli 17, C.P. 1010 (Franco Slataper), 34132

Udine—via Stringher 14 (Federico Tacoli), 33100

Uget-Torino—galleria Subalpina 30, Piazza Castello, Torino (Leo Ussello), 10123

Varese—via Speri della Chiesa Jemoli 12 (Giuseppe Santoni), 21100

Venice—San Marco 1672 (Claudio Varsolato), 30124

Vercelli—via Stara 1 (Giuseppe Conti), 13100

Verona—Stradone Scipione Maffei 8 (Benito Roveran), 37100

Vicenza—Contrà Reale 12 (Piero Fina), 36100

Viterbo—c/o Liberia Quatrini, via della Sapienza 7 (Giuseppe Lupattelli), 01100

APPENDIX E

TOURING CLUB ITALIANO OFFICES

The Touring Club Italiano has nearly 1,000 offices and numerous representatives throughout Italy. Many of these only offer regional or local information and road assistance. For general information on Italy and TCI publications, visit one of the larger offices listed below. When writing for information, maps or publications, address inquiries and orders to the central office—also headquarters of the Touring Bicycle Club—in Milan.

Milan: Corso Italia 10, 20122
Turin: Via C. Alberto 57, 10121
Rome: via Ovidio 7/a, 00193
Bari: Via Melo 259, 70121

APPENDIX F

ITALIAN CANOE CLUBS & ASSOCIATIONS

AOSTA VALLEY

Canoa Club Montebianco, Via Vodince 44, 11100 Aosta.

PIEDMONT

Canoa Club Alessandria c/o Leo Vannelli, Via Benedetto Croce 15, 15100 Alessandria.
Canoa Club Cuneo, Via XX Settembre 30, 12100 Cuneo.
Gruppo Canoe Fossano c/o Walter Fochi, 12045 Fossano.
Canoa Club Torino c/o Domenico Ravizza, Via S. Giulia 5, 10124 Torino.
Canoa Club Ivrea, Vicolo S. Grato 1, 10015 Ivrea.
Canoa Club Valsesia c/o Azienda di soggiorno e turismo, Corso Roma 38, 13019 Varalle Sesia.

LOMBARDY

CUS Pavia, Via Faramelli 20, 27100 Pavia.
Vigevano Canoa Club, Via Trieste 13/14, 27029 Vigevano.
Società Canottieri Ticino, Lungoticino E. Calfi, 27100 Pavia.

Canoa Club Bergamo c/o Roberto Faletti, Via Manara 7, 24100 Bergamo.
Canoa Club Valtellina c/o Dario Cesaroni, via Don Guanella 4, 23100 Sondrio.
Società Canottieri Adda, Via Nazario Sauro 16, 20075 Lodi.
Gruppo Canoe Crema, 26013 Crema.
Adda Canoe c/o Vergani, Via Verdi 8, 20060 Basiano.
Canoa Club Cassano d'Adda, 20062 Cassano d'Adda.

LIGURIA

Canoa Club Ventimiglia, Val Roia c/o Renato Gizzoni, Via S. Bernardo 10/9, 18012 Bordighera.
Canoa Club Lerici c/o Wladimiro Farina, Via Garibaldi 63, 19030 La Serra.

TRENTINO ALTO-ADIGE

Canoa Club Trento, Via Fratelli Fontana 1, 38100 Trento.
Sport Club Merano, C.P. 35, 39012 Merano-Meran.
Canoa Club Bressanone—Sportverein Milland c/o Stampler Hans, Angerweg 9, 39042.
Kayak Club Rienz, 39030 Chienes-Kiens.
Sportverein Sterzing c/o A. Toni, Via Città Nuova 20, 39049 Vipiteno-Sterzing.

VENETO

Canoa Club Castelfranco Veneto c/o Lino Dal Maso, Via Volta 8, 31033 Castelfranco Vento.
Canoa Club Valstagna 3 c/o U. Cacioppo, 36020 Valstagna.
Canoa Club Vadobbiadene c/o P. Brunelli, Via Cordana 11, 31049 Valdobbiadene.
Gruppo Canoe Valcellina, Via Giordani 7, 33080 Claut.
Canoa Club Udine c/o Duilio De Vit, Via A. Malignani 19, 33100 Udine.
Kayak Club Natisone c/o Reza Ali, Via Libertà 90, 33044 S. Giovani al Natisone.

EMILIA ROMAGNA

Canoa Club Bobbio c/o Lomberdi, Corso Garibaldi 20, 29022 Bobbio.

Canoa Club Valtrebbia, C.P. 58, 29100 Piacenza.

Canoa Club Parma, Via Solari 15, 43100 Parma.

U.I.S.P. Parma, Viale Balsetti 12, 43100 Parma.

Canoa Club Romagna c/o Paolo Ruffini, Via Garibaldi 30, 48012 Bagnacavallo.

Gruppo Appennino Canoe, Via Caduti di Casteldebole 12, 40132 Bologna.

TUSCANY

Canoa Club Val di Magra c/o Franco Giuselini, Galleria Michelangelo, 54011 Aulla.

Canoa Club Pistoia c/o Marco Vannucchi, Via Monte Sabotino 47, 51100 Pistoia.

Canoa Club Arezzo c/o Circoscrizione di Quaranta, 52100 Arezzo.

Canoa Club Ombrone, Istia di Ombrone, 58040 Grosseto.

Canoa Club Sahara Siena c/o Roberto Polizzy, Via M. Orlandi 19, 53100 Siena.

Canoa Club F.O.C.A. c/o Moreno Formica, Via Della Libertà 3, 61030 Lucrezia.

Canoa Club Valmetauro c/o L. Desanti, Via De Gasperi, 61034 Fossombrone.

MARCHES

Canoa Club Vallesina c/o Franco Mancinelli, Via Rinaldi 15, 60035 Iesi.

UMBRIA

Canoa Club Orvieto, Via Sette Martiri 72, 05019 Orvieto Scalo.

Gruppo Canoe Terni c/o Carlo Pandozy, Via Sanzio 21, 05100 Terni.

LATIUM

Gruppo Canoe Roma c/o Giorgio Carbonara, Via T. Valfrè 12, 00165 Roma.
Canoa Club San Giorgio al Liri, 03047 San Giorgio al Liri.
Canoanium Club Subiaco c/o Daniele Mariano, 00028 Subiaco.

ABRUZZI

Canoa Club Vomano c/o Palestra Olympia, Via Badia 34, 64100 Teramo.

CAMPANIA

Canoa Club Volturno, Via Alviani 12, 81043 Capua.
Canoa Club Napoli, Castello di Baia, 80070 Bacoli (NA)
Canoa Club Policastro c/o Domenico Russo, 84067 Policastro Bussentino.

BASILICATA

Gruppo Canoe Lucano c/o Savino Di Leva, Via Roma 106, 85024 Lavello.

SICILY

Kayak Club Zingaro Palermo c/o Beppe Grifeo, Via C. Nigra 15, 90141 Palermo.
Canottieri Siracusa Sez. Canoa, Via Testaferrata 22, 96100 Siracusa.

SARDINIA

Canoa Club Cagliari c/o Roberto Caredda "Lo Sportivendolo", Corso Vittorio Emanuele 181, 09100 Cagliari.

APPENDIX G

USEFUL TERMS AND CONVERSIONS

PRONUNCIATION GUIDE

```
a ........................................."a" as in car
e.........................................."e" as in let
i ........................................."ee" as in feel
o ........................................."o" as in open
u ........................................."oo" as in moon
ci ......................................."chee" as in cheese
ce........................................"che" as in chess
chi ......................................pronounced key
che ....................................."cke" as in ticket
gi.......................................pronounced "gee"
ge........................................"je" as in jelly
gh...........................(before e and i) "g" as in go
gl....................(before e and i) "lli" as in stallion
gn......................................."ni" as in bunion
sc...................(before e and i) pronounced as "sh"
```

NUMBERS

```
1.........................................uno
2.........................................due
3 ........................................tre
```

```
  4.....................................quattro
  5......................................cinque
  6.........................................sei
  7.......................................sette
  8........................................otto
  9........................................nove
 10.......................................dieci
 11......................................undici
 12......................................dodici
 13......................................tredici
 14...................................quattordici
 15.....................................quindici
 16.......................................sedici
 17....................................diciassette
 18.....................................diciotto
 19....................................diciannove
 20........................................venti
 30.......................................trenta
 40......................................quaranta
 50.....................................cinquanta
 60.....................................sessanta
 70.....................................settanta
 80......................................ottanta
 90......................................novanta
100.......................................cento
500....................................cinquecento
1,000....................................mille
10,000.................................diecimila
100,000................................centomila
```

DAYS OF THE WEEK

```
Monday ......................................Lunedi
Tuesday .....................................Martedi
Wednesday .................................Mercoledi
Thursday.....................................Giovedi
Friday ......................................Venerdi
Saturday.....................................Sabato
Sunday ....................................Domenica
```

MONTHS

January	Gennaio
February	Febbraio
March	Marzo
April	Aprile
May	Maggio
June	Giugno
July	Luglio
August	Agosto
September	Settembre
October	Ottobre
November	Novembre
December	Dicembre

GENERAL SUBJECTS

Good morning	Buon giorno
Good evening	Buona sera
Good night	Buona notte
Goodbye	Arrivederci
How are you?	Come sta?
Fine, thank you	Bene, grazie
Hope I see you soon	Spero di riverderla presto
Do you speak English?	Parla inglese?
I don't understand	Non capisco
Yes/No/Please	Si/No/Per favore
Thank you	Grazie
You are welcome	Prego
Excuse me	Mi scusi
Yesterday	ieri
Today	oggi
Tomorrow	domani
The day after tomorrow	dopodomani
Morning	mattina
Noon	mezzogiorno
Afternoon	pomeriggio
Evening	sera
Night (Midnight)	notte (mezzanotte)
What time is it please?	Che ore sono per favore?

It is .... o'clock .... Sone le. ...

A.M./P.M. .... di mattina/di pomeriggio

How is the weather this morning? ....

.... Com'e il tempo questa mattina?

It is sunny/rainy/cold/hot ....

.... C'e sole/sta piovendo/fa freddo/fa caldo.

Where is the bus stop? .... Dov'e la fermata dell'autobus?

Does this bus go to. ... ? .... Questo autobus va a. ... ?

Can you tell me when to get off? ....

.... Mi puo dire quando devo scendere?

POST OFFICE (Ufficio Postale)

Stamps .... francoboli

Air Mail. .... via aerea

Special delivery. .... espresso

Registered mail .... raccomandata

Post Card. .... cartolina postale

Telegram .... telegramma

What is the postage for this letter? .... Quanti francoboli
per questa lettera?

BANK (Banca)

Money (paper money) .... denaro (banconote)

Small change .... moneta

Traveller's checks. .... assegno di viaggio

What is the rate of exchange? .... Quant'e il cambio oggi?

I have U.S. dollars .... Ho dollari statunitensi

ACCOMMODATIONS (Alloggio)

Bed. .... letto

Blanket .... coperta

Dining room .... sala da pranzo

Heat. .... riscaldamento

Key .... chiave

Hotel. .... albergo

Manager .... direttore

Pillow. . . . . .cuscino
Shower. . . . . .doccia
Do you have a single (double) room with bath?. . . . .
. . . . .Avete una camera singola (doppia) con bagno?
I don't like this room. . . . . .Non mi piace questa camera.
What is the price?. . . . . .Quanto costa?
Is breakfast included? . . . . .E inclusa la colazione?
At what time is dinner?. . . . . .A che ora e la cena?
I would like to phone this number . . . .
. . . . .Vorrei telefonare a questo numero.
I will be staying three nights . . . . .Restero tre notti.
There is no hot water . . . . .Non c'e acqua calda.

ON THE TRAIL

Archaeology. . . . . .archeologia
Backpack . . . . .zaino
Bicycle . . . . .bicicletta
Boots . . . . .stivali
Bridge. . . . . .ponte
Canoe. . . . . .canoa canadese
Camping . . . . .campeggio
Cave. . . . . .grotta
Excursion . . . . .gita
Fauna. . . . . .fauna
Flora. . . . . .flora
Fly. . . . . .volo
Guide . . . . .guida
Horse/horseback . . . . .cavallo/cavalcata
Hut. . . . . .rifugio
Insects. . . . . .insetti
Knife . . . . .coltello
Lake . . . . .lago
Map. . . . . .mappe
Mountain . . . . .montagna
Mountain climbing. . . . . .alpinismo
Mountain farm. . . . . .malga
Mountain hut. . . . . .casera
Nature . . . . .natura

```
Park . . . . . . . . . . . . . . . . . . . . . . . . . . . . . . . . . . . . . . . . . . .parco
Pass/saddle between mountains . . . . . . . . . . . . . . . . . .forcella
Rain coat . . . . . . . . . . . . . . . . . . . . . . . . . . . . . .impermeabile
Refuge. . . . . . . . . . . . . . . . . . . . . . . . . . . . . . . . . . . . . . .rifugio
Regulations. . . . . . . . . . . . . . . . . . . . . . . . . . . . . . . . . .regole
Rescue . . . . . . . . . . . . . . . . . . . . . . . . . . . . . . . . . . . .soccorso
River. . . . . . . . . . . . . . . . . . . . . . . . . . . . . . . . . . . . . . . .fiume
Rock . . . . . . . . . . . . . . . . . . . . . . . . . . . . . . . . . . . . . . . .roccia
Rope . . . . . . . . . . . . . . . . . . . . . . . . . . . . . . . . . . . . . . . .corda
Route indicator. . . . . . . . . . . . . . . . . . . . . . . .segnalazioni
Sleeping bag . . . . . . . . . . . . . . . . . . . . . . . . . . .sacco a pelo
Ski. . . . . . . . . . . . . . . . . . . . . . . . . . . . . . . . . . . . . . . . . . .sci
Snow. . . . . . . . . . . . . . . . . . . . . . . . . . . . . . . . . . . . . . . .neve
Speleology. . . . . . . . . . . . . . . . . . . . . . . . . . . .speleologia
Survival . . . . . . . . . . . . . . . . . . . . . . . . . . . .sopravvivenza
Tent . . . . . . . . . . . . . . . . . . . . . . . . . . . . . . . . . . . . . . . .tenda
Trail/path. . . . . . . . . . . . . . . . . . . . . . . . . . . . . . .sentiero
Trek . . . . . . . . . . . . . . . . . . . . . . . . . . . . . . . . . . . . . . . . .trek
Volcano. . . . . . . . . . . . . . . . . . . . . . . . . . . . . . . . . .vulcano
Water . . . . . . . . . . . . . . . . . . . . . . . . . . . . . . . . . . . . . .acqua
Tire . . . . . . . . . . . . . . . . . . . . . . . . . . . . . . . . . . . . . . . .ruota
```

DINING

```
Bread. . . . . . . . . . . . . . . . . . . . . . . . . . . . . . . . . . . . . . .pane
Breakfast . . . . . . . . . . . . . . . . . . . . . . . . . . . . .colazione
Cheese. . . . . . . . . . . . . . . . . . . . . . . . . . . . . . . .formaggio
Chicken . . . . . . . . . . . . . . . . . . . . . . . . . . . . . . . . . . .pollo
Coffee. . . . . . . . . . . . . . . . . . . . . . . . . . . . . . . . . . . .caffè
Dinner . . . . . . . . . . . . . . . . . . . . . . . . . . . . . . . . . . . .cena
Lunch . . . . . . . . . . . . . . . . . . . . . . . . . . . . . . . . . . .pranzo
Meat . . . . . . . . . . . . . . . . . . . . . . . . . . . . . . . . . . . . .carne
Menu . . . . . . . . . . . . . . . . . . . . . . . . . . . . . . . .menu/list
Mineral water . . . . . . . . . . . . . . . . . . . . . . .acqua minerale
Pasta dishes. . . . . . . . . . . . . . . . . . . . . . . . .pastascutta
Pepper . . . . . . . . . . . . . . . . . . . . . . . . . . . . . . . . . .peppe
Restaurant . . . . . . . . . . . . . . . . . . . . . . . . . . .ristorante
Salad . . . . . . . . . . . . . . . . . . . . . . . . . . . . . . . . . .insalata
Salt . . . . . . . . . . . . . . . . . . . . . . . . . . . . . . . . . . . . . . .sale
```

Snack . . . . .spuntino
Sugar. . . . . .zucchero
Tea . . . . .tè
Wine. . . . . .vino
We are not ready to order yet . . . .
. . . . .Non siamo ancora pronti per ordinare.
I would like a salad. . . . . .Vorrei un'insalata.
The bill please. . . . . .Il conto per favore.

EMERGENCY

Ambulance . . . . .ambulanza
Firemen . . . . .pompieri
First Aid . . . . .pronto soccorso
Help! . . . . .Aiuto!
Hospital . . . . .Ospedale
Police . . . . .polizia
Police station . . . . .commissariato
I lost my passport. . . . . .Ho perso il mio passaporto.
They stole my wallet . . . . .Mi hanno rubato il portafoglio.

METRIC CONVERSION

Linear Measure

1 cm. = 0.394 in.
1 m. = 3.280 ft./1.094 yds.
1 km. = 0.621 mile
1 in. = 2.54 cm.
1 ft. = 0.305 m.
1 yd. = 0.914 m.
1 mile = 1.609 km.

Weights and Capacity

1 ounce = 0.030 liter
1 cup = 0.236 liter
1 pint = 0.473 liter
1 quart = 0.946 liter
1 gallon = 3.785 liters
1 liter = 1.056 quarts

1 ounce = 28.35 grams
1 pound = 453.592 grams
1 gram = 0.0353 ounce
1 kilogram (1000 grams) = 2.205 pounds

TEMPERATURE CONVERSION

From Fahrenheit to Celsius: Fahrenheit temperature, minus 32, divided by 1.8.

From Celsius to Fahrenheit: Celsius temperature, times 1.8, plus 32.

ADVENTURE GUIDES

WALKER'S BRITAIN 336 pp. $12.95
CYCLIST'S BRITAIN 304 pp. $12.95
BIRDWATCHER'S BRITAIN 256 pp. $12.95
WALKING THROUGH SCOTLAND 192 pp. $10.95
WALKING THROUGH WALES 172 pp. $10.95
WALKING THROUGH THE LAKE DISTRICT
    224 pp. $10.95
WALKING THROUGH NORTHERN ENGLAND
    208 pp. $10.95
*WALKING IN AUSTRIA 192 pp. $10.95
*WALKING IN THE ALPS 192 pp. $9.95
*WALKING IN SWITZERLAND 205 pp. $9.95
*WALKING IN NORTHERN FRANCE 192 pp. $8.95
THE MOUNTAINS OF GREECE: A WALKER'S GUIDE
    176 pp. $12.95
WALKS & CLIMBS IN THE ENGADINE 192 pp. $12.95
WALKS & CLIMBS IN THE PYRENEES 206 pp. $12.95
TRAMPER'S GUIDE TO NEW ZEALAND 243 pp. $12.95

These can be found at the best bookstores or you can order directly. Send your check (add $2.50 to cover postage & handling) to:

HUNTER PUBLISHING, INC.
300 RARITAN CENTER PARKWAY
EDISON NJ 08818

Write or call (201) 225 1900 for our free color catalog describing these travel books and many more.

*These titles are available in the UK from Moorland Publishing Co. Ltd.

Hundreds of other specialized travel guides, maps, and language courses on cassette are available from Hunter Publishing. Among those that may interest you:

ITALY

*FLORENCE & TUSCANY VISITOR'S GUIDE
160 pp. $8.95
*THE ITALIAN LAKES VISITOR'S GUIDE 240 pp. $10.95
CHARMING SMALL HOTELS OF ITALY 192 pp. $9.95
BACKPACKING & WALKING IN ITALY 224 pp. $11.95

Plus

HUGO'S ITALIAN PHRASEBOOK 128 pp. $3.25
HUGO'S ITALIAN IN THREE MONTHS
CASSETTE COURSE $29.95
An intensive course in idiomatic and conversational speech. Accompanying a 24-lesson book are 4 hours of audio tapes designed to teach pronunciation and speed learning. Takes the absolute beginner to a good working knowledge of the language. Packed in a molded vinyl case which fits easily on a bookshelf. Eight other languages are also offered in the series.

FRANCE

HISTORIC HOUSES, CASTLES &
GARDENS OF FRANCE 376 pp. $15.95
FRANCE ON BACKROADS 256 pp. $12.95
*BRITTANY VISITOR'S GUIDE 160 pp. $8.95
*THE LOIRE VISITOR'S GUIDE 160 pp. $8.95
*NORMANDY VISITOR'S GUIDE 160 pp. $8.95
*THE SOUTH OF FRANCE
VISITOR'S GUIDE 160 pp. $8.95
EPERON'S FRENCH WINE TOUR 256 pp. $12.95